# A SAINSBURY COOKBOOK

# THE COOKING OF
# SOUTHERN INDIA

## RAFI FERNANDEZ

HYDERABAD

ANDHRA
PRADESH

KARNATAKA

Bangalore

Mysore

KERALA

Madras

TAMIL
NADU

Alleppey

Cape Comorin

# CONTENTS

Published exclusively for J Sainsbury plc
Stamford House  Stamford Street
London SE1 9LL
by Woodhead-Faulkner (Publishers) Ltd
Fitzwilliam House  32 Trumpington Street
Cambridge CB2 1QY

First published 1987
Text, photographs and illustrations
© J Sainsbury plc 1987

Printed in Great Britain

# THE AUTHOR

Rafi Fernandez was born in India but has lived in England since she was twenty-one, working first for a travel agency and then for an airline. The latter position enabled her to travel to many parts of the world, and so to develop an interest in a wide range of cooking.

In 1983, after attending a cookery seminar, Rafi began to organise her own catering events on the theme of 'West meets East through Food', at which she introduced eastern customs and culture related to the menu being served. Her first book, on Malaysian Cookery, was written at the encouragement of her Malaysian Indian husband; more recently she has written a book on Indian vegetarian cooking. Rafi now teaches Indian Cookery at the Hedingham Adult Centre in Essex, and is still always keen to develop new culinary ideas, including those brought home by her husband who travels extensively in his work.

Rafi lives in the country with her husband and two sons Kevin and Lee. Her second main hobby is growing unusual plants using seeds and bonsais from different parts of the world.

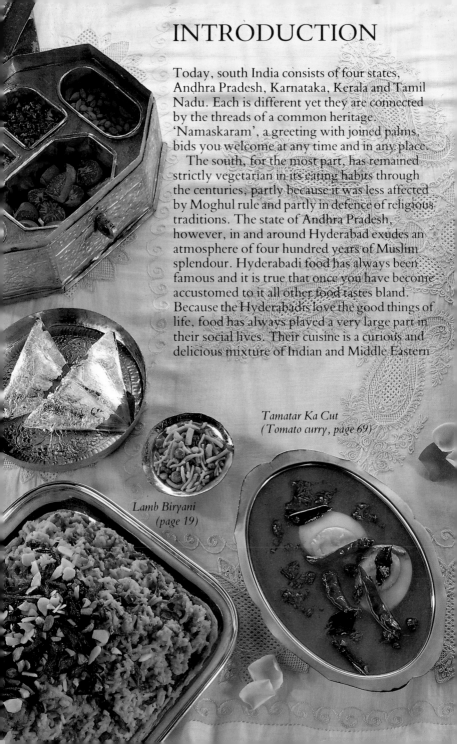

# INTRODUCTION

Today, south India consists of four states, Andhra Pradesh, Karnataka, Kerala and Tamil Nadu. Each is different yet they are connected by the threads of a common heritage. 'Namaskaram', a greeting with joined palms, bids you welcome at any time and in any place.

The south, for the most part, has remained strictly vegetarian in its eating habits through the centuries, partly because it was less affected by Moghul rule and partly in defence of religious traditions. The state of Andhra Pradesh, however, in and around Hyderabad exudes an atmosphere of four hundred years of Muslim splendour. Hyderabadi food has always been famous and it is true that once you have become accustomed to it all other food tastes bland. Because the Hyderabadis love the good things of life, food has always played a very large part in their social lives. Their cuisine is a curious and delicious mixture of Indian and Middle Eastern

*Tamatar Ka Cut*
*(Tomato curry, page 69)*

*Lamb Biryani*
*(page 19)*

cooking. It is still claimed that the best Hyderabadi food can only be found in the old bazaars of the *Char Minar*, 'the four minarets', a Moghul building where in the tiny cave-like shops spicy moghlai food is cooked by men whose fathers and grandfathers passed down the precious recipes. Moghlai cuisine specialises in rich, spicy meat dishes: an old saying affirms that you cannot be a good Muslim unless you 'eat meat and lots of it'. Meat, chicken and rice are the principal ingredients of the majority of moghlai preparations. Rich pilaus, fragrant biryanis and kebabs in infinite variety are some of the delicacies. After the decline and fall of the Moghul empire, their traditions and customs spread to Hyderabad where the last Moghul emperor Aurangezeb ended his days. The Moghuls' cuisine has not only been jealously guarded and faithfully maintained in Hyderabad but polished and perfected to a pitch of refinement which the Moghuls themselves had not known.

*Kachoombar (Onion and tomato salad, page 86)*

*Faluda (Gelatine pudding, page 90)*

*Pasinday (Pan-cooked lamb kebabs, page 43)*

*Nan Bread (page 27)*

*Kirakai Pudina Pacchhadi (Yogurt with cucumber and mint, page 84)*

5

I was born in Secunderabad but lived in Hyderabad for ten years before emigrating to the United Kingdom and with nostalgia I am including in each section of this book recipes I thoroughly enjoy. I hope when you have tried some or all you will realise that Hyderabad deserves its reputation for gourmet food which is rich, spicy and exceptionally delicious.

From Karnataka I chose the Coorg cuisine. Coorg, the land of lush paddy fields and verdant mountain ranges with coffee, oranges and cardamoms is well known for its hospitality. A house in Coorg or a Coorg's home anywhere is an open house and a well laid out table with appetising food is the rule. Within minutes of the guest's arrival, the lady of the house busies herself preparing a meal. She does not consider it a big task to produce a meal of chicken curry, rice, chutney, a salad and a sweet within no time. Her pleasure lies in seeing her guests fed very well, whatever the time of day or night.

Though Coorg is famous for its coffee, oranges and cardamoms, rice is the staple food, and, as a result, most of the popular dishes are rice-based. Rice also plays a prominent role on auspicious days or feasts and festivals and a Coorg bride is always welcomed by her in-laws for the first time by the ritual of being made to kick a heap of raw rice on the threshold, thus spilling rice everywhere and bringing with her prosperity for her new family.

Kerala was officially mapped only in 1956, although its people have lived there for centuries. Kerala lures foreign adventurers constantly as it has a convenient coastline and a treasury of spices. Although my husband was born in Malaysia, many of his family still live in Kerala and it is from their kitchens that I selected dishes to represent Kerala. My in-laws are Catholics, speaking Malayalam, the language of Kerala. They are chiefly fisher-folk and naturally excel in seafood dishes. Chemmeen Kari (Kerala prawn curry, page 52), Meen Molee (Fish in coconut milk, page 58), and Chemmeen Achar (Pickled prawns, page 54) are authentic recipes which have been passed down the generations, though I have reduced the quantities of chillies, as the amounts they use are enough to take your palate off. Also in Kerala there is a very small community of the original 'white' Jews. They are an isolated community with roots dating back to the time of St Thomas the Apostle's voyage to India in AD 52. Those still living in India are direct descendants and have never intermarried into any Indian communities. I have chosen two of their dishes: Hamim Broath (Stuffed chicken, page 35) and Imhasa (Stuffed vegetables, page 76).

Tamil Nadu is greatly influenced by tradition, customs and religion. Family ties are strong and even today traces of ancient orthodox behaviour and habits are noticeable in many homes. Hospitality is a social custom which is given prime importance in every household, irrespective of social status. People in Tamil Nadu enjoy entertaining guests with sumptuous feasts, especially on festival days. Even those who cannot afford to serve a lavish meal believe in sharing what little they have with their guests. A guest in a Tamil Nadu household is welcomed with a 'shombu' (a pot) of cold water. This relieves the weary traveller, who drinks a little of it to quench his thirst and washes his face and feet. After this there is a mutual exchange of news and the guest is then invited to share a meal. A traditional Tamil Nadu meal is served on a tender banana leaf. Again this has a significance: it is related to orthodox customs and considered a symbol of cleanliness and hygiene. Every guest is asked to take a seat on a rectangular wooden plank and the feast is served on the leaf. Tamil Nadu boasts of its hospitality and welcomes you to enjoy it. In the old scriptures it is written 'Do better than your fellow men, be hospitable to your guests and to the needy; your happiness lies in seeing them happy'. I have chosen some of their favourites like Puliyodora (Tamarind rice, page 28), Kuttu (Mixed vegetables, page 70) and Pacchhadi, a yogurt-based accompaniment with many variants like Kirakai Pudina Pacchhadi (Yogurt with cucumber and mint, page 84), and Pal Payasam (Rice pudding, page 90) which is served at many famous Indian temples as a *prasadam* to the resident deities. A *prasadam* is any item of food which is offered first to the deities and then to the priests and pilgrims, free of charge.

Having done a gastronomic survey of Indian cuisine I found the south Indian dishes the most mouthwatering: even a Spartan would find them impossible to resist. Spicing is the chief factor, ranging from the two or three of the cheaper types used by the poorer people to the eight or ten or more exotic spices used in the more elaborate dishes. From time immemorial India has been known as the land of spices, and the south has always been famous for cardamoms and cinnamon, saffron and cloves, pepper and nutmeg, ginger and chillies.

*Masala* – the blending of various spices – is the cornerstone of all Indian cookery and especially of south Indian cookery. The *masalas* are freshly ground every day on a flat grinding stone with a stone pestle (you can of course use your electric food processor or an electric coffee mill). So important are the *masalas* that in many south Indian communities a bride stands on a grinding stone for some of the wedding ceremonies. The stone and pestle are always included as a vital part of the possessions a new bride takes with her to her husband's home. In Coorg a miniature version of the grinding stone is placed in a baby girl's crib with the blessing 'may you live a hundred years like the stone'.

South Indian food has a reputation for being very 'hot', and Madras reputedly has the most hot, but I have reduced the chilli to quantities that should be palatable. Those who can take the 'hotness' can increase the chilli quantities to suit their own tastes.

It is a fallacy, moreover, that all south Indian foods are vegetarian. The adventurous gastronome will find that a number of 'fleshy delights' are also served the traditional way, on the ubiquitous banana leaf. A lavish range of non-vegetarian dishes is offered in tiny restaurants that have sprung up like mushrooms everywhere. The south is famed for its temples, its Kancheepuram silks, and its dances – the *Bharata Natyam*, dances relating stories of the deities by movements of eyes, head, hands and feet, and the *Kathakali*, the elaborate dance-drama of Kerala, with its stylised costumes and masks and its heavy make-up – but you cannot really be said to have glimpsed the heart of the south until you have tasted its food.

'Curry' comes from the south Indian term *kari*, although 'curry' is the best known but most maligned export of Indian cuisine. An Indian *kari*, the genuine article, is prepared from a combination of spices, condiments and coconut, freshly ground and sautéed in oil or ghee and then cooked until the gravy thickens; no extraneous thickening agent is ever used. To this is added chicken or fish or meat or vegetables as one wishes.

The evolution of south Indian cuisine is a story of romantic tradition, of much ritual and of superb artistry. The south has perfected a skill with spices to transform often bland and tasteless materials into superb dishes. 'Food is God' the ancient Sanskrit scriptures avow. So let us pay south Indian cuisine the supreme compliment of a surfeited guest: 'there is no reply to such a meal'.

## Equipment and utensils

To perfect the art of south Indian cooking you do not need to invest in new utensils and equipment. Ordinary saucepans are adequate or a large, heavy-based frying pan with a lid, although a wok or a *karai*, which is similar to a wok, would be very useful as they can be used for any type of cooking. Many Indian breads and pancakes are roasted and for this we use a *tava*. This is a heavy metal griddle and a good quality one lasts a lifetime. You can use a Scottish 'girdle' or a cast-iron frying pan. An electric blender is a vital piece of equipment as so many recipes call for ingredients to be ground or blended. When grinding or blending in an electric blender, add oil to facilitate the action. This acts as a lubricant and will prolong the life of the blender. An electric coffee mill is a good alternative.

## Cooking with spices

**Dry-roasting:** when whole spices need to be ground I recommend that they are dry-roasted first. Heat a griddle or a heavy frying-pan and fry each spice individually, without oil, until fragrant. Roasting the spices brings out their flavour as well as making the grinding easier.

**Addition of spices when cooking:** always reduce the heat before adding any ground spices as they burn very easily which will give your dish a bitter taste. If you are worried about burning the spices, use my method. I mix ground spices like coriander, cumin, turmeric and chilli powder in a little water and fry them gently until the water has evaporated and the oil has separated from the spices.

**'Final fry' (tarka or baghar):** this is a technique used mostly in lentil and vegetable dishes to give them extra zest. In a pan which rests firmly on the cooker, heat the oil until nearly smoking and fry the whole spices until they begin to crackle. Standing well back, hold the lid of the main pan in one hand and pour the oil and spices on to the vegetables or lentils and cover the pan immediately, to retain the aroma. When the hot oil touches the lentils or vegetables there is a slight splash, like a tiny explosion. It is not at all dangerous and is one of the delights of Vedic cooking.

**Hot curries:** I have used chilli powder and/or dried and fresh chillies in most of the recipes, but the quantity used (unless the dish is meant to be hot as most of the pickles and chutneys are) should be palatable to all. Serve natural yogurt as an accompaniment: this will act as a 'fire extinguisher'. Drinking water with your meal will cool your mouth. If your curry has become too hot, temper it with lemon juice or sugar and serve plain rice or an Indian bread to absorb some of the chilli taste.

# Indian ingredients

**Asafoetida (hing):** a dried resin sold in block or powder form. It has an acrid and bitter taste and should be used sparingly. Keep it tightly sealed as it has a strong smell. Stores indefinitely.

**Browned onions:** these make a lovely garnish and have a delicious taste. They are used in many recipes in this book. Deep-fry thinly-sliced onions in hot oil until they are evenly brown and crisp. Drain them on sheets of absorbent paper, allow them to cool completely and store indefinitely in air-tight jars.

**Cardamom (elaichi):** the 'queen of spices'. Green and white varieties are used in both savoury and sweet dishes. Seeds from these varieties can be chewed to freshen the mouth. Black cardamoms are also available and are larger but only used in cooking. All varieties store well.

**Chillies, fresh (hari mirch):** have become indispensable in Indian cuisine for their pungent taste. They are rich in vitamins A and C. Fresh red chillies (*lal mirch*) are not as pungent as green ones. Both can be frozen without blanching. Care should be taken in preparation as the seeds in particular are very hot, and contact with the eyes should be avoided. You may wish to wear rubber gloves and remove the seeds under running water.

**Chillies, dried (sukhi mirch):** are always dark red in colour but vary in size and strength. The bigger the chilli, the less pungent it is. Whole dried chillies are mainly used in vegetable and lentil dishes.

**Chilli powder (mirch ki bhukni):** commercially packaged chilli powders vary in strength and you may need to adjust the quantities accordingly. Stores well but it is a good idea to buy only small quantities at a time.

**Cinnamon (dalchini):** available in sticks (quills) and ground. When cinnamon is used whole in my recipes I have given the length of the stick, not the thickness. Discard it before serving, or warn your guests of its presence in the dish! Stores indefinitely.

## Grinding/ pulverising

*When grinding or blending wet ingredients like onion, ginger, garlic, chillies and coriander leaves, use oil to facilitate the action of the blender. As I use ginger and garlic daily I save time by pulverising batches of 500 g (1 lb) at a time and storing them in the freezer in small, airtight jars. Thawed portions will keep for up to seven days in the refrigerator. As a rough guide, 1 teaspoon garlic paste is the same as 4 whole cloves, and 1 teaspoon ginger paste is equivalent to a 5 cm (2-inch) piece.*

**Clove (lavang):** used in both savoury and sweet dishes. Available whole and ground. Stores indefinitely.

**Coconut milk (nariyal doodh):** this can be obtained from fresh coconut or desiccated coconut, but coconut cream blocks are readily available and will save you a lot of time. Soak 75 g (3 oz) chopped cream coconut and a pinch of salt in 175 ml (6 fl oz) hot water. Stir till dissolved, and your *thick* coconut milk is ready. For *thin* coconut milk, use only 25 g (1 oz) creamed coconut. Adjust the quantities according to each recipe, using these proportions.

**Coriander seeds (dhaniya):** available whole and ground. Used to thicken and add flavour to curries.

**Coriander leaves (kotmir or hara dhaniya):** available in bunches. Leaves are added to *masalas* (page 8) or used as a garnish. Can be open-frozen whole or frozen as crushed pulp. Thawed portions will keep for up to seven days if refrigerated.

**Cumin (zeera):** white cumin seeds are sweet and aromatic. Available whole and ground. The black variety *(shahzeera)* is more aromatic. Both varieties store indefinitely.

**Curry leaves (kariyapath):** curry leaves are aromatic and have an earthy flavour. Fresh curry leaves can be open-frozen. Dried leaves are best stored in a wicker basket. Both fresh and dried leaves should be discarded during eating.

**Fennel seeds (sonf):** fennel has a delicious aroma and a sweet and agreeable taste. Available whole and in powdered form. Both store indefinitely.

**Fenugreek (methi):** fenugreek has a pungent and slightly bitter taste. Use sparingly. Available in whole and powdered form. Stores indefinitely.

**Five-spice powder (wu hsiang wen):** a blend of star anise, fennel, cinnamon, clove and Szechuan pepper. When a recipe calls for ground cinnamon, cardamom and cloves, use this as a substitute. Stores indefinitely.

**Garam masala:** a fragrant mixture of spices like cardamom, clove, cinnamon, nutmeg and so

on. Many varieties are available but a homemade batch is definitely better.

25 g (1 oz) peeled cardamom seeds
40 g (1½ oz) cloves
40 g (1½ oz) cinnamon
40 g (1½ oz) black peppercorns
1 whole nutmeg, crushed

Individually dry-roast each spice until fragrant (page 10). Cool and then grind to a fine powder in an electric blender or a coffee grinder. Store indefinitely in an airtight jar, marking the label with the spices you have combined for easy reference.

**Ghee (clarified butter):** a very popular cooking medium in India. Ghee is made by melting butter in water until the water has evaporated. In south India it is used for all religious and auspicious occasions. In this country, Sainsbury's concentrated butter can be used in place of ghee.

**Ginger/garlic powder:** a small jar of these powders is always useful for those 'just in case' moments. Dried garlic flakes are also available.

**Gram flour (besan or channa atta):** flour made from split peas. Make your own by dry-roasting split peas without burning them and grinding them in a coffee grinder. Sieve and store in an airtight jar. 'Besan' has a distinctive flavour but wheatflour or wholemeal flour can be used as a substitute.

**Kewra:** an essence extracted from a variety of screwpine *(pandanus odoratissimus)*. It is available as a concentrated essence of which only a few drops are required, and also as kewra water, which is diluted and has a milder flavour. Stores indefinitely. It is mainly used in sweet dishes and you can use rose-water or essence as a substitute.

**Mace and nutmeg (javithri or jaiphul):** obtained from the same tree. Mace is the dried thin covering of the fruit and the dried kernel is the nutmeg. Available whole and ground. Both store indefinitely.

**Poppy and sesame seeds (khus khus and til):** mainly used in curries which require a thicker consistency; also sprinkled on several Indian breads. These seeds are difficult to grind to a fine powder or paste. I recommend you dry-roast them a little longer than the other ingredients and grind them first on their own before adding the other ingredients. This will give the poppy and sesame seeds more chance to break up. In India, sesame oil *(til-ka-tel)* is popularly used in cooking.

**Pulses (gram or dhal):** gram is the whole seed and dhal is the gram split into halves and husked. The most popular are black gram (urad, urad dhal); mung beans (green gram, mung dhal); red lentils (tuvar or arhar dhal), which are always sold split and are the most commonly used pulse in India, especially in the south; and Bengal gram (channa dhal, of which chick-pea is a variant). Always have some varieties in your larder, stored in airtight jars in a cool, dark place.

**Rice (chawal):** rice is south India's staple food. For daily use, cook patna or long-grained rice but for special occasions and dishes like pilau or biryani use basmati.

**Sambhar powder:** a useful blend of spices which it is convenient to have in store. This quantity will make enough for four or five recipes.

5 tablespoons chilli powder
5 tablespoons ground coriander
3 tablespoons fenugreek seeds, dry-roasted and ground
1 teaspoon mustard seeds, dry-roasted and ground

Pass through a sieve to mix evenly. Store in an airtight jar.

**Sinapsis or mustard seeds (rye):** small, round and darkish-brown or greyish-brown in colour. The seeds are odourless but when they are pounded and moistened they have a bright yellow colour. In India, mustard seeds are fried in oil with cumin seeds and curry leaves and are used to season vegetables and lentil dishes in their final stages of cooking, (see page 10).

**Tamarind (imli):** fruit from the tamarind tree, which is a native of south India. Processed pods are sold in packets and as purified concentrated pulp. Prepared juice is also now available.

**Shopping**
*To purchase spices by mail order, write to Viniron Ltd., 119 Drummond Street, London NW1 2HL.*

15

Tamarind juice *(imli pani)* is extensively used in south Indian cooking for its sweet–sour taste. To prepare tamarind juice soak a fistful of tamarind (the size of a golfball) in 5 tablespoons hot water until pulpy and then vigorously squeeze out the juice through a fine sieve or a piece of muslin. If a recipe calls for a larger quantity of tamarind juice, adjust the quantities accordingly. Concentrated tamarind is now available. Follow the same method but use only 1 teaspoon of the concentrated pulp. Malt vinegar or lemon juice can be used in place of tamarind juice and in roughly the same proportions, but this will not provide the same cooling properties as tamarind.

**Turmeric (haldi):** turmeric is obtained from the roots of a plant which belongs to the ginger family. Available dried in whole or ground form. The taste and smell of turmeric are aromatic and pungent. The yellow dye is very strong and stains materials, so avoid spilling any curries containing it.

**Warq:** not an ingredient but a traditional garnish of silver and gold leaf. It is sold backed by wax-paper: to use, place on the food waxpaper side up, and peel off the waxpaper to leave the sheet behind.

**Wheatflour (atta):** in India, wheatflour is obtained by grinding wheat grains in a flour mill or in a stone grinder *(chakki)*. Use wholemeal flour as a substitute.

**Yogurt:** used as both an ingredient and an accompaniment. Its bland, slightly tart taste complements spicy dishes. Yogurt is known as curd in India and is commended by Vedic scriptures dating back five thousand years. It is also especially associated with Lord Krishna who is known as *Govinda Gopala*: a friend of cows and lover of curd and buttermilk.

**Zaffron/Saffron (zaffran):** the world's most expensive spice, available in strands and ground form. When a dish requires authentic saffron flavour use only the strands. To use, soak a few strands in warm milk or water. Never substitute turmeric for saffron.

# RICE AND BREADS

In south India, freshly boiled rice in unlimited quantities is served four times in a meal, each time to be eaten with a different course. Therefore, I call it 'Rice Unlimited & Co.'! First, a few drops of melted ghee are sprinkled over the rice; this purificatory ritual has been practised since the Vedic period (c. 1500–450 BC) and rice is considered the most important ingredient because of Vedic scriptures. Because most Indians eat rice at least once a day, there is a seemingly infinite variety of ways to cook it. Breads are more popular in the north, but the south has certain favourites too and they are all delicious. They are not served several at a time, but as soon as the diner finishes one hot bread, another one appears and so on until he acknowledges he can eat no more.

## CHAWAL OR SADAM

Plain boiled rice                                         Serves 4–6

Preparation time: 25 minutes + 30 minutes soaking

*350 g (12 oz) patna, basmati or American long grain rice*

*600 ml (1 pint) water*

*1 teaspoon butter or vegetable or olive oil*

*salt to taste*

*Although many people in the West find rice difficult to cook, this method has never failed me. In south India, rice is the staple food for many millions and accompanies all curries.*

Pick and wash the rice thoroughly in three or four changes of water or until the water remains clear. Allow it to soak for about 30 minutes to get a better yield and fluffier cooked grains. Drain well and put the rice in a heavy pan which has a tight-fitting lid. Add the measured water, salt and butter or oil. Bring to the boil on a high heat. When it reaches the boil, reduce the heat to the lowest possible setting, cover the pan and allow to simmer till the rice is cooked. This usually takes 15–20 minutes, but depends on the rice. If your lid does not fit tightly, cover the pan with a sheet of foil as well as the lid as it is essential to prevent any steam escaping. To check if your rice is cooked, lift the lid a little and peep to see if small steam holes have formed on the surface. If they have, close the lid again immediately, turn off the heat and allow the rice to rest for about 5 minutes before serving.

To serve, use a flat spoon, pushing it down to the base and lifting the rice out from the bottom rather than in layers which would damage the delicate cooked grains. Once you have transferred a section to the serving plate, gently loosen the grains.

*Variation: Bagare Chawal* First sauté the rice in the butter or oil with ½ teaspoon black cumin seeds, 2.5 cm (1-inch) cinnamon quill and two green cardamoms. Then add the water and salt and proceed as for Chawal or Sadam.

When dishes call for cooked rice, prepare this well in advance and cool it, particularly if it has to be stir-fried, to prevent the rice grains sticking together. Rice can be reheated in a microwave oven. Cover the bowl with cling film and heat on full power for about 3 minutes. Alternatively, place the rice in a sieve, cover and steam for about 10 minutes.

# DOSAI

Fermented pancakes                                    Makes 10–12

Preparation time: 40 minutes + 8 hours soaking + 12 hours fermenting

75 g (3 oz) black gram
(urad dhal)

175 g (6 oz) patna or long
grain rice

concentrated butter, ghee or
vegetable oil

salt to taste

*These can be eaten as a snack with chutney, or as a main dish with the addition of a lentil curry or Alu Sag (Potato curry, page 83). I have also served them with chicken or meat curries and I always make sure there is one spare for me to have hot with a dab of ghee and sugar.*

Soak the dhal and rice separately in water for about 8 hours or preferably overnight. Drain the dhal and reserve the water. Drain the rice. In an electric blender, grind first the dhal and then the rice to a smooth paste, using a little of the dhal water, if necessary, to facilitate grinding. Mix the pastes and add enough dhal water to make a

batter of pouring consistency (as single cream).
Cover the bowl and leave it overnight to
ferment. Ensure a large enough bowl is used to
allow the increase in volume.

If the batter is too thick the next day, add the
required amount of water. Then heat a heavy,
flat griddle which has a lid and brush it with ghee
or oil (in India we pass a piece of muslin dipped
in oil over the griddle for each dosai). When the
griddle is nearly smoking hot add a ladle of the
batter and quickly spread it out thinly with the
back of the ladle, using circular movements
from the inside to the outside. Cover with a lid.
When the edges begin to curl in 1–2 minutes,
put a little ghee or oil on the griddle around the
sides of the pancake and gently ease it off with a
flat metal spatula. Turn it over and cook the
other side for the same length of time.

To keep them warm till serving time wrap
them in a tea towel or a sheet of greased foil, but
keep the delay to a minimum. Do not freeze.

## LAMB BIRYANI

Preparation time: 30 minutes + 2 hours cooking
+ 30 minutes soaking                                      Serves 4–6

|  |
| --- |
| 2.5 cm (1-inch) piece of fresh ginger |
| 6 cloves of garlic |
| 1 teaspoon chilli powder |
| ½ teaspoon ground turmeric |
| 1 kg (2 lb) lamb neck fillet, cut in large pieces |
| oil for deep-frying |
| 4 large onions, sliced very finely |
| 625 g (1¼ lb) basmati rice, picked, washed and soaked for 30 minutes |
| 900 ml (1½ pints) water |
| 250 ml (9 fl oz) natural yogurt, beaten |

*After many hundreds of years, Hyderabadis still gaze
with the same rapture at their city, and eat biryani as if
they have never eaten it before: the city is famous
throughout India for its biryanis. I have chosen Lamb
Biryani but Hyderabad offers a range made from
mutton, chicken, fish or prawns and even quail,
partridge and wild duck. To prepare a good biryani,
many factors need to be considered, therefore follow
my recipe carefully to avoid any mishaps.*

Blend the ginger, garlic, chilli powder, ground
turmeric and salt to taste to a paste. Rub the paste
well into the meat pieces and keep aside. In a
wok or a large pan, heat the oil and fry the
onions till they are deep brown and crisp.
Remove with a slotted spoon on to absorbent
paper and allow to cool, reserving the oil.

Reserving a handful for garnish, crush the

250 ml (9 fl oz) milk

a handful each of coriander and mint leaves, chopped

4 green chillies, de-seeded if wished and chopped

½ teaspoon cardamom seeds, crushed

juice of 1 lemon

a few strands of saffron, soaked in 4 tablespoons hot milk or water

125 ml (4 fl oz) hot water

a little concentrated butter or ghee

salt to taste

onions and add them to the lamb pieces and mix well. In a separate pan put the rice in the water with some salt and bring it to the boil once; then drain off the water and set it aside. Take a large, heavy saucepan which has a tight-fitting lid and add four tablespoons of the oil in which you have fried the onions. Evenly cover the base and put a layer of meat at the bottom. Mix the yogurt, milk, half the coriander and mint leaves, all the chillies, cardamom seeds and lemon juice together. Sprinkle half of this mixture over the meat. Then spread half the rice over the meat. Sprinkle the rest of the coriander and mint leaves over the rice. Layer all the remaining meat over the rice and pour in the second half of the yogurt mixture. Make the last layer with the rest of the rice. Make deep holes with the handle of a wooden spoon or a chopstick and into each hole pour a little of the dissolved saffron. Sprinkle the water over the top layer of rice and add a few small pieces of concentrated butter or ghee.

Cover the pan with a cloth or a sheet of foil and then the lid. Weight the lid down if possible (I use a another pan filled with water). Place the pan on the lowest heat (use a heat diffuser if your heat cannot be easily controlled) and allow the biryani to cook until the meat and rice are done. Check after 25–30 minutes by pinching a few grains of rice or pushing a knife through: it should come out clean. If it is not cooked and all the water has been absorbed sprinkle on a little more hot water and leave to cook, tightly re-covered. While checking, work fast as you should not allow too much steam to escape.

Before serving, gently mix the rice and meat and garnish with the reserved browned onions. Hyderabadis also top this with nuts and the silver and gold sheets known as warq (page 16). Serve this with Ande Ka Salan (Egg curry, page 31) and Kirakai Pudina Pacchhadi (Yogurt with cucumber and mint, page 84).

*Lamb Biryani*

# DADHYODHANA

Curd rice                                                    Serves 4–6

Preparation time: 30 minutes + 30 minutes soaking

350 g (12 oz) patna,
basmati or American long
grain rice

600 ml (1 pint) water

1 teaspoon butter or
vegetable or olive oil

½ a fresh coconut, grated,
or 8 tablespoons desiccated
coconut

3 green chillies, de-seeded if
wished

2.5 cm (1-inch) piece of
fresh ginger

a handful of coriander
leaves, chopped

500 g (1 lb) carton of
natural yogurt, beaten

1 tablespoon concentrated
butter or ghee or vegetable
oil

1 teaspoon mustard seeds

6 curry leaves, chopped

salt to taste

*The news of the first pregnancy of a Coorg girl is
celebrated by presenting her with 'koopadis' or food
parcels of curd rice with a spoon or knife concealed
inside them. She chooses one parcel and if a spoon is
found it is presumed her baby will be a girl and if a
knife is picked it will be a boy. Indians believe that
pregnant girls always have a craving for sour foods.*

Pick and wash the rice thoroughly in three or
four changes of water or until the water remains
clear. Leave it to soak for 30 minutes; then drain
it well and put it in a pan with the measured
water, salt to taste and butter or oil. Cover the
pan and bring it to the boil on a high heat, and
then reduce the heat and allow it to simmer for
15–20 minutes. Meanwhile, blend the coconut,
chillies, ginger and coriander to a fairly coarse
texture in an electric blender. Add salt to taste to
the yogurt and fold in the blended ingredients.
Heat the ghee or oil in a small frying pan and fry
the mustard seeds and curry leaves till the seeds
crackle. Pour the oil and seasoning ingredients
on the yogurt. Mix well, and then cool and fold
gently into the cooked rice.

  This rice is served cold and you can enhance it
by tossing in small cubes of cucumber or green
(unripe) mango. Freezing is not recommended.

# MOONG KITCHDI

Rice with split green gram (mung beans)                      Serves 4–6

Preparation time: 45 minutes + 30 minutes soaking

350 g (12 oz) patna or long
grain rice, picked and
washed

175 g (6 oz) split mung
beans

*My mother often prepares this for breakfast and serves
it with eggs freshly fried in ghee. It can be served with
any curries and accompaniments and if you cook it
with a little extra water it makes a pleasant soup
served with natural yogurt for someone feeling poorly.
In India it is served to guests who have over-stayed*

6 tablespoons vegetable oil

1 medium-size onion, sliced finely

2.5 cm (1-inch) piece of fresh ginger, sliced finely

2 cloves of garlic, sliced finely

2 green chillies, de-seeded if wished but left whole

½ teaspoon ground turmeric

1 litre (1¾ pints) water

salt to taste

*their welcome as it symbolizes that the hostess is running out of rice and has to combine other ingredients to make it stretch further, but it is also cooked when someone in the house is ill.*

Wash the rice and mung beans together and allow them to soak for 30 minutes. Heat the oil in a heavy pan with a tight-fitting lid and fry the onion until it becomes translucent. Add all the spices and garlic with salt to taste and cook on a low heat until aromatic. Drain the rice and beans, add to the pan and sauté for 5 minutes. Add the measured water and bring it to the boil. Reduce the heat to the lowest setting and cover the pan with a sheet of foil and then the lid. Allow to simmer for 20–25 minutes or till the rice and mung beans are fluffy. Open the pan once after about 10 minutes and give everything a gentle stir to prevent the green gram rising to the top, but work fast to avoid loss of steam from inside the pan. Serve hot as above or have it as a light snack with natural yogurt, hot mango pickle and a tossed green salad.

# POORIES

Deep-fried unleavened bread                    Makes 20–24

Preparation time: 40 minutes + 1 hour resting

350 g (12 oz) wheat flour or wholemeal flour

1 teaspoon salt

water

oil for deep-frying

Make the dough as for Chappatis (page 26), allow it to rest and divide it into 20–24 portions. Make balls and roll them out as chappatis, keeping the remaining dough covered so it does not dry out. Heat enough oil for deep-frying, and when it is nearly smoking fry one poori at a time, encouraging them by tapping the edges with a wooden spatula to make them puff out. Stack the fried poories in a colander lined with absorbent paper to drain off any excess oil. Keep them covered to retain the heat. Serve hot. Indians have formulated a rhythm when rolling out chappatis and poories: we roll out and cook simultaneously and you can acquire this talent if you practice a few times. Freezing is not recommended for poories.

# IDLIS

Preparation and cooking time: 30 minutes + 8 hours soaking
+ 12 hours fermentation

275 g (9 oz) patna or long
grain rice, picked and
washed

175 g (6 oz) black gram
(urad dhal), picked and
washed

1 teaspoon fenugreek seeds
(optional)

a pinch of bicarbonate of soda

oil for greasing

salt to taste

*These are served throughout the day at south Indian
vegetarian restaurants with Sambhar (Lentil curry
with vegetables, page 64) and chutney. A famous
temple in Kanchipuram prepares a masala version,
but instead of small cakes makes one large one, which
is cut into small pieces and offered free of charge to the
devotees. I have an idli-making pan which steams
twelve cakes simultaneously, but you can use a non-
stick egg poaching pan.*

Soak the rice and black gram with the fenugreek
seeds if you are using them for 6–8 hours or
preferably overnight. Drain well, reserving the
water and grind them in a food processor with
the bicarbonate of soda and salt to taste, adding
some of the soaking water to enable you to grind
everything to a smooth consistency. Remove
the mixture to a large bowl, cover it with a damp
cloth and allow it to rest for 10–12 hours in a
warm place like an airing cupboard. During this
time fermentation will take place and make the
mixture swell and become more liquid, so ensure
your bowl is large enough to accommodate this
increase.

   Mix the batter well and check the consistency,
which should be of double cream. If it is thicker
add the required amount of water. Oil the
depressions of an idli-tray or poaching pan well,
pour spoonfuls of the batter into each depression
and steam them for 10–15 minutes. Serve hot.
To keep prepared idlis warm, wrap them in a
sheet of greased foil and leave in a warm oven.
They should not be frozen.

   *Variation:* Add a finely chopped onion, 2 finely
chopped green chillies, de-seeded if wished, a
handful of chopped coriander leaves, a pinch of
ground asafoetida and ground pepper to the
batter after fermentation and then steam as above.

*Chappatis* ►
*Idlis (Steamed rice cakes)*
*Poories (Deep-fried
unleavened bread)*

24

# CHAPPATIS

350 g (12 oz) wheat flour or wholemeal flour, plus extra for rolling

1 teaspoon salt

water

oil for greasing

concentrated butter or ghee, melted

*Rice and Chappatis or Poories (see page 23) are prepared daily for all the meals and these act as vehicles for the curries. Usually Chappatis or Poories are eaten first with a vegetable dish and the remaining meal – which might consist of a meat, poultry or fish dish, a lentil dish and another vegetable – is completed with rice. If you are planning both rice and Chappatis or Poories allow two per person.*

Sieve the flour and salt into a large mixing bowl, holding the sieve as high as you can to allow air to pass through the falling flour. Gradually add water to make a soft and pliable dough. Cover and allow to stand for about 1 hour.

Grease the palms of your hands with oil and vigorously knead the dough for five minutes on a clean work surface, or use the dough hook of a food processor. Divide the dough into 10–12 equal portions. Make a ball out of each and flatten it out on a lightly floured board or surface. Roll out using semi-circular movements to a circle about 18 cm (7 inches) across, keeping the rest of the dough covered so it does not dry out. Heat a heavy griddle until smoking hot and cook the chappatis on each side until brown spots appear. Brush immediately with ghee or butter and serve hot.

To keep chappatis warm, wrap them in a sheet of foil and leave the packet on the griddle or if the waiting period is longer place the packet in a warm oven. Prepared chappatis can be stacked in a foil packet and frozen. To use, thaw them and then warm them in the oven, without unwrapping them, for 15 minutes.

# NAN BREAD

(Pictured on page 5)                                        Makes 8

Preparation time: 40 minutes + 1½ hours resting
+ 10 minutes baking

|  |
| --- |
| 1 teaspoon fresh or dried yeast |
| 4 tablespoons warm water |
| 1 teaspoon sugar |
| 500 g (1 lb) plain flour, plus extra for kneading |
| ½ teaspoon baking powder |
| ½ teaspoon salt |
| 150 ml (¼ pint) milk |
| 150 g (5.29 oz) carton of natural yogurt, beaten |
| 1 egg |
| 25 g (1 oz) butter, melted, plus extra for greasing |

**To glaze:**

| |
| --- |
| 1 egg yolk |
| 1 tablespoon poppy or onion seeds |

**Oven temperature:**
Gas Mark 8/230°C/450°F

*In India, Nan is traditionally baked in a clay oven which we call a 'tandoor'. They are just as delicious when baked in an ordinary oven and a must when dishes like Pasinday (page 43) or Shami Kebabs (page 44) are served.*

In a small bowl, sprinkle the yeast over the warm water, leave it for a few minutes to soften and then stir to dissolve. Add the sugar and leave aside until frothy, about 10 minutes. Sift the flour, baking powder and salt together. Heat the milk until it is lukewarm. Remove from the heat and add the yogurt, yeast, egg and melted butter. Make a well in the flour and gradually pour in the milk mixture; mix to combine it thoroughly until you have a smooth dough. Knead the dough for about 10 minutes until it is springy. Sprinkle on a little dry flour if the dough is sticky to handle. Cover the bowl with cling film and leave it in a warm place until the dough doubles in bulk and a finger pushed into the dough leaves an impression. This may take 1–1½ hours or longer depending on the warmth around the bowl. Preheat the oven with two ungreased baking trays in it.

Divide the dough into eight portions and roll them into balls. Dip your palms in dry flour and flatten each ball into a teardrop shape by tossing it from one palm to the other and gently pulling it on one side. Keep the centre thinner than the rim. Brush them with the egg yolk and sprinkle them with poppy or onion seeds. Remove the hot trays and lightly grease them. Quickly place four nans on each tray and return them to the oven. Bake the nans for 10 minutes or until golden and puffed. To obtain the traditional spots which appear on these nans when baked in a clay oven, place them under a preheated grill for 1 or 2 minutes. Serve hot. Keep them wrapped in a kitchen towel if there is a delay in serving and keep them warm in a low oven until you are ready to serve.

# PULIYODORA

Tamarind rice                                            Serves 4–6

Preparation time: 30 minutes + 30 minutes soaking

350 g (12 oz) patna, basmati or American long grain rice

600 ml (1 pint) water

1 teaspoon butter or vegetable or olive oil

6 tablespoons sesame or vegetable oil

1 teaspoon mustard seeds

1 teaspoon fenugreek seeds

1 teaspoon sesame seeds

5 large dried chillies, de-seeded and broken coarsely

4 curry leaves, chopped coarsely

2 tablespoons chick-peas or bengal gram

¼ teaspoon ground asafoetida

1 teaspoon ground turmeric

125 ml (4 fl oz) tamarind juice

salt to taste

*Puliyodora has many variations, according to each region. I have chosen the one which I tasted at a renowned temple in the Tirupathi Hills. A lady paying homage to the deity with Puliyodora kindly gave me the recipe.*

Pick and wash the rice thoroughly in three or four changes of water or until the water remains clear. Leave it to soak for 30 minutes; then drain it well and put it in a pan with the measured water, salt to taste and the butter or oil. Cover and bring to the boil on a high heat and then reduce the heat and allow to simmer for 15–20 minutes. Meanwhile, heat the oil on a medium heat and fry the mustard seeds. When they crackle add the fenugreek seeds, sesame seeds, dried chillies, curry leaves and chick-peas or bengal gram. Sauté until the fenugreek seeds swell and the gram is golden brown. Reduce the heat to medium and add the ground asafoetida and turmeric. Reduce the heat to low and add the tamarind juice and salt. Bring to the boil and then simmer till the mixture thickens. When the rice is cooked, cool it slightly, transfer to a large mixing bowl and gently loosen the grains. Add the tamarind juice mixture and toss the rice gently to coat the grains evenly. Serve cold or if you wish warm it gently.

*Note:* Puliyodora can be highlighted by adding freshly grated coconut, peanuts and cashew nuts to the boiling tamarind juice. The chilli taste is distinctive, so adjust it to suit you.

# POULTRY AND EGG DISHES

When I left India in 1965 we were still purchasing live chickens and cleaning them at home. Today we have advanced and can buy cleaned chickens. The chickens are never too large and their fat content, in comparison with those we buy here, is very low. Until recently chicken was cooked for special occasions only but with modern technology fast taking over chicken now ranks equal to lamb in popularity.

Eggs are still an expensive ingredient in India and the old-fashioned method of purchasing eggs still exists in some areas: eggs are immersed in water and if they float they are fresh and if they sink they are not.

## KOZHI THALI

Coorg-style chicken fry                                    Serves 4–6

Preparation time: 25 minutes + 40 minutes cooking

| |
|---|
| 1.5 kg (3 lb) chicken, jointed |
| 1 teaspoon ground turmeric |
| 6 tablespoons desiccated coconut |
| 3 green chillies, de-seeded if wished |
| 5 cloves of garlic |
| 2.5 cm (1-inch) piece of fresh ginger |
| 2 teaspoons ground coriander |
| 1 teaspoon ground cumin |
| ¼ teaspoon ground cloves |
| ½ teaspoon ground cinnamon |

*Between June and September the Coorgi men put away their hunting weapons and concentrate on farming. When the farming is done they indulge in 'shikar' (shoot) and before the first 'shikar' weapons are cleaned and offered 'puja' (prayers). This feast is called 'keilpodu' and Kozhi Thali is amongst the festive dishes they prepare. They would use a special kind of home-made vinegar which they add to all non-vegetarian curries. Malt vinegar mixed with tomato purée is an excellent substitute. Dadhyodhana (Curd rice, page 22) is usually served with this.*

Place the chicken joints in a mixing bowl, rub them with ground turmeric and salt to taste and set aside. Dry-roast the desiccated coconut till it is golden-brown in colour. In an electric blender, grind together the chillies, garlic, ginger, ground spices, coriander leaves and

29

| |
|---|
| *a handful of coriander leaves* |
| *4 tablespoons vegetable oil* |
| *2 medium-size onions, sliced finely* |
| *1 teaspoon freshly ground black pepper* |
| *1 teaspoon malt vinegar mixed with ½ teaspoon tomato purée* |
| *salt to taste* |

coconut to form a fine paste. Then heat the oil in a large, heavy frying pan and fry the onions until they are golden brown. Reduce the heat and add the ground paste. Fry until the mixture is aromatic and the oil has separated. Add the chicken and keep frying until all the pieces are evenly coated and of one colour. Cover the pan and cook the chicken on a low heat until done, about 40 minutes. Occasionally stir the chicken and if necessary add a little hot water. When the chicken is almost done, add the pepper and the vinegar mixture. This dish should be dry so if there is any excess liquid leave the pan uncovered and quickly reduce the liquid on a high heat.

# ANDE KA KAGINA

Spicy scrambled eggs                                    Serves 4

Preparation time: 15 minutes

| |
|---|
| *1 tablespoon concentrated butter or ghee* |
| *1 small onion, chopped finely* |
| *1 green chilli, chopped finely* |
| *a few fresh coriander leaves, chopped* |
| *1 firm tomato, chopped finely* |
| *¼ teaspoon ground turmeric* |
| *4 large eggs (size 1–2), beaten with 4 tablespoons water* |
| *salt to taste* |

*This is very popular in the south and is particularly favoured by the Muslims and the Christians; it is delicious for breakfast or as a snack with freshly made toast. It also makes a lovely filling for vol-au-vents or cocktail savouries. As a young girl I often filled my sandwiches for school lunch with this and even though by the time I ate them they were cold, they were still delicious with hot tea from my flask.*

Heat the butter or ghee gently in a non-stick frying pan or a wok and fry the onion lightly. Add the remaining ingredients except the eggs and stir-fry for 1 minute. Add the eggs and cook slowly, stirring all the time to break up any large lumps. Serve hot.

Alternatively, make two or four omelettes or 'chilas' by mixing all the ingredients in a bowl first. My mother often wrapped these omelettes in chappatis for my lunch box or gave them to us when we went on picnics. I introduced this to my English friend Ros who joined me on a trip to India, and she could not believe how an omelette could taste so lovely even when eaten cold. Freezing is not recommended.

# ANDE KA SALAN

Egg curry                                                    Serves 4–6

Preparation time: 20 minutes + 20 minutes cooking

4 tablespoons vegetable oil

1 large onion, sliced finely

4 cloves of garlic, crushed

5 cm (2-inch) piece of fresh ginger, crushed

2 tablespoons ground almonds

1 teaspoon chilli powder or to taste

1 teaspoon ground turmeric

1 teaspoon ground coriander

a little water

2 large dry red chillies, de-seeded if wished

398 g (14 oz) can of chopped tomatoes

6 curry leaves or 2 bay leaves

25 g (1 oz) creamed coconut dissolved in 175 ml (6 fl oz) boiling water

6 large hard-boiled eggs (size 1–2), halved lengthways

salt to taste

**To garnish:**

thin slices of green or red pepper or coriander leaves and flaked almonds

*I usually serve this curry with Biryani (page 19) and Kachoombar (Onion and tomato salad, page 86) but it is just as delicious with plain boiled rice and any vegetable curry. My young son does not like eggs, especially the yolk. The only way he will eat eggs from this curry is by giving me the yolk and filling the scoops with natural yogurt and then challenging his brother to see who can place the whole half of the egg in his mouth.*

Heat the oil in a large pan or a wok and fry the sliced onion until golden brown. Mix the garlic, ginger, ground almonds, chilli powder, turmeric and coriander with a little water to form a paste. Reduce the heat and add the spice paste and whole dry chillies. Fry gently until the oil separates from the spices. Add the tomatoes, curry leaves or bay leaves, coconut milk and salt to taste and allow to simmer until you have a thick gravy, about 15 minutes. Check the seasoning and add the eggs, keeping the yolks upwards. Cover the eggs with the gravy and simmer for about 5 minutes. Serve hot, garnishing with either thin slices of red and green peppers or coriander leaves and almond flakes. Ande Ka Salan does not freeze well.

# KOZHI VARUVAL

Tamil Nadu chicken                                             Serves 4–6

Preparation time: 15 minutes + 2 hours resting
+ 30 minutes frying per batch

20 large dry red chillies

½ teaspoon cumin seeds

¼ teaspoon fennel seeds

2 tablespoons coriander seeds

2.5 cm (1-inch) piece of fresh ginger

1 kg (2 lb) boneless, skinless chicken breast

juice of 1 lime or lemon

vegetable oil for shallow-frying

salt to taste

**To garnish:**

crisp lettuce leaves

slices of tomatoes, beetroot and onions

lemon or lime wedges

*I have followed this recipe strictly without reducing the chilli quantity. If you wish either de-seed the chillies or reduce the quantity for your first attempt. Serve as a starter with salad or as part of a main meal.*

First soak the chillies in warm water for five minutes and, meanwhile, dry-roast the cumin, fennel and coriander seeds. Then grind the chillies, roasted spices and ginger to a fine paste, using some of the chilli-soaking water to facilitate grinding if necessary. Cut the chicken into bite-size pieces. Mix the lemon or lime juice, salt and ground paste and marinade the chicken pieces in it for about 2 hours.

Heat the oil in a wok or a large frying pan and fry the chicken pieces with the marinade on a medium heat until cooked, about 30 minutes. Do not overcrowd the pan; you should have a single layer frying at a time to cook the chicken evenly. Keep each fried batch warm in a gently heated oven. To serve, cover your serving platter with lettuce leaves. Place the chicken pieces on it and garnish with slices of tomatoes, beetroot, onions and lemon or lime wedges.

*Chicken Mulligatawny Anglo-Indian Style*

*Ande Ka Salan*
*(Egg curry)*

*Kozhi Varuval ( Tamil Nadu chicken)*

# CHICKEN MULLIGATAWNY ANGLO-INDIAN STYLE

Preparation time: 15 minutes
+ 1 hour cooking

Serves 4–6 as main meal
or 8–10 as soup

1.5 kg (3 lb) oven-ready chicken

1.2 litres (2 pints) chicken or vegetable stock

1 onion, sliced finely

200 g (7 oz) tomatoes, chopped

2 cloves of garlic, crushed

5 cm (2-inch) piece of fresh ginger, crushed

2.5 cm (1-inch) stick of cinnamon

8 curry leaves

1 teaspoon each of ground coriander, cumin and fennel

½ teaspoon ground turmeric

6–8 fenugreek seeds

250 ml (9 fl oz) thick coconut milk

1 onion, finely sliced and deep-fried till brown and crisp

juice of 1 lemon

a few coriander leaves

salt to taste

*A large number of Anglo-Indians live in Cochin and they originally adopted and adapted the traditional 'rasam' (pepper water), a south Indian favourite, into this meat-based soup. Britons returning from India brought this back to England but it has been adapted further and what one now considers 'mulligatawny' in England is closer to oxtail soup in character.*

Place the chicken in a large heavy pan and add the stock, sliced raw onion, tomatoes, garlic, ginger, cinnamon, curry leaves, ground spices, fenugreek seeds and salt to taste. Bring to the boil and then allow to simmer until the chicken is tender, 45 minutes–1 hour. Remove the chicken to a large platter or chopping board. Carefully joint it and keep aside. Strain the stock and return the chicken pieces to it. Add the coconut milk and simmer for about 5 minutes. Just before serving add the deep-fried onion, lemon juice and coriander leaves.

# HAMIM BROATH

Jewish-style stuffed chicken                    Serves 4–6

Preparation time: 20 minutes + 30 minutes soaking + 1½ hours cooking

*175 g (6 oz) patna, basmati or American long grain rice*

*½ teaspoon butter or vegetable or olive oil*

*900 ml (1½ pints) water*

*250 g (8 oz) lean lamb, cut into small pieces*

*6 tablespoons concentrated butter or ghee*

*2 firm red tomatoes, chopped*

*1 teaspoon garam masala*

*½ teaspoon ground turmeric*

*1.5 kg (3 lb) oven-ready chicken*

*2 onions, chopped finely*

*salt to taste*

*A Jewish friend of mine in England often prepares this just using chicken necks. I find it easier to use a whole chicken and this is how it is still prepared in India by the few 'white' Jews (last count seventy) still living in the state of Kerala.*

Wash the rice and soak it for 30 minutes. Drain it, add the butter or oil and 400 ml (14 fl oz) water and bring quickly to the boil in a pan with a close-fitting lid. Simmer for 15–20 minutes on a reduced heat and then allow the rice to cool. Cook the lamb in the remaining 500 ml (18 fl oz) water until tender, about 30 minutes. Drain it, reserving the water. In a separate pan, heat half the ghee or butter and fry the meat pieces until they are evenly browned. Add the tomatoes, garam masala, salt to taste and half the turmeric. Add half the rice and mix well. Stuff the chicken with this mixture and truss it in the normal way. In a large pan heat the remaining ghee or butter and fry the onions until golden brown. Add the remaining turmeric and a pinch of salt. Add the stuffed chicken and leftover rice. Cover the pan and cook it on a very low heat until the chicken is tender, about 45 minutes. Sprinkle on a little of the reserved lamb stock if necessary, to stop the rice sticking.

# MURG-E-MUSSALAM

Stuffed Muslim chicken                                    Serves 4–6

Preparation time: 30 minutes + 3 hours resting + 1½ hours cooking

*1 teaspoon freshly ground black pepper*

*1½ teaspoons salt*

*1.5 kg (3 lb) oven-ready chicken*

*1 onion, sliced finely and deep-fried until golden brown and crisp*

*25 g (1 oz) fresh ginger, ground to a paste*

*150 g (5.29 oz) carton of natural yogurt*

*6 tablespoons concentrated butter or ghee*

*2 onions, sliced finely*

*25 g (1 oz) almond flakes*

*25 g (1 oz) sultanas*

*juice of 2 limes or lemons*

*4 small potatoes, boiled and chopped coarsely*

*4 hard-boiled eggs, chopped coarsely*

*350 ml (12 fl oz) hot water*

**Oven temperature (optional):**
*Gas Mark 3/180°C/350°F*

*Id-uz-Zuha (Bakri Idd) is observed by the Muslims to commemorate the offer of Prophet Ibrahim (Abraham) to sacrifice his son. Prayers are offered and goats and sheep are sacrificed. My family make this dish with a whole goat or sheep but as this isn't very practical I have used a chicken.*

Rub pepper and salt on the chicken and prick it all over with a fork. Crush the deep-fried onion and mix it with the ginger paste and yogurt. Rub this mixture evenly over the chicken and allow it to marinade for about 3 hours. Preheat the oven if you are using it.

In a large, heavy pan with a tight-fitting lid, heat half the ghee or butter and brown the onion slices. When the onions are golden brown add the almond flakes and sultanas. Fry until the sultanas swell up. Add the lime or lemon juice, potatoes, and eggs and stir-fry for 1 minute. Remove from the heat. Stuff the chicken with this mixture and either tie the chicken or stitch it.

Heat the remaining ghee or butter in the same pan and sauté the chicken on all sides until the skin turns to a golden colour. Cover the chicken with a sheet of foil if your lid is not tight-fitting, add the water, and leave to simmer gently until the chicken is done, 1–1½ hours. If you wish you can cook it in a heavy casserole in a preheated oven, allowing about 15 minutes per pound of chicken.

Partridge, quail or pheasant can also be prepared in this way, allowing one partridge or quail per person and one pheasant for two persons. This recipe is not suitable for freezing.

*Murg-E-Mussalam (Stuffed Muslim chicken)*

# MURGH KA SALAN

Preparation time: 30 minutes + 1 hour cooking

4 tablespoons vegetable oil

2.5 cm (1-inch) stick of cinnamon

4 green cardamoms, bruised

4 cloves

4 black peppercorns

1 star anise

2 onions, sliced finely

5 cm (2-inch) piece of fresh ginger, crushed finely

6 cloves of garlic, crushed finely

1 tablespoon ground coriander

1 teaspoon ground cumin

1 teaspoon ground turmeric

chilli powder to taste

a little water

1.5 kg (3 lb) oven-ready chicken

2 tablespoons tomato purée

25 g (1 oz) creamed coconut, crumbled

salt to taste

**To garnish:**

coriander leaves

flaked almonds

*This is definitely my own style although influenced by the Muslims and Telegu Hindus of Hyderabad. It is a favourite of my sons and I always prepare a little extra as they love to have the leftovers with fried eggs and fresh toast for breakfast.*

Heat the oil on a high heat in a large, heavy pan and fry the whole spices until aromatic. Add the onions and fry them until they are golden-brown. Reduce the heat a little and add the ginger and garlic and fry until the raw smell disappears. Mix the ground spices including the chilli powder with salt to taste into a paste with a little water. Reduce the heat further and add the spice paste. Stir-fry until the water has evaporated and the oil begins to separate from the spices. Using a heavy cleaver, cut the chicken into bite-size pieces, including the bone. Add the chicken pieces to the pan and continue to stir-fry until all the pieces are evenly browned. The whole spices may be discarded now or after the chicken is fully cooked. Cover the pan and leave to simmer for 30 minutes. Juices released from the chicken should be sufficient to cook the chicken but check and if necessary sprinkle on a few drops of hot water. After 30 minutes, add the tomato purée and coconut and mix well. This curry should have a nice thick gravy but if you prefer it lighter mix up to 125 ml (4 fl oz) hot water with the coconut before adding it. Check for seasoning and leave to simmer until the chicken is fully done which should take another 15–30 minutes. Garnish with coriander leaves and flaked almonds. Serve with plain boiled rice or any bread.

# MEAT DISHES

In the early stages of Indian civilization, our ancestors were non-vegetarians: the Aryans of the Vedic period welcomed a distinguished guest with 'fatted calf' hospitality. In India today there are a variety of attitudes to meat. Through religious changes over hundreds of years there are certain doctrines that lead to the prohibition of beef eating for Hindus, as the cow is recognised as a direct descendant of Kamadhanu, a sacred spirit with the face of a beautiful woman. Consequently its milk is highly valued and its life protected. Total vegetarianism was adopted by the Hindus much later through the teaching of non-violence. For the Muslims consuming pork is forbidden as it has been described as an unclean animal in the Holy Quran. Other meat they consume must be 'halal' a special slaughter stipulated in the Quran. The Jews abide by their 'kosher' laws.

## ATTU ERACHI CHOPS

Madras-style lamb chops                                    Serves 4–6

Preparation time: 15 minutes + 40 minutes cooking

| 12 lamb chops |
| --- |
| ¼ teaspoon aniseed |
| ¼ teaspoon poppy seeds |
| ¼ teaspoon cumin seeds |
| 10 black peppercorns |
| 2 cloves of garlic |
| 2.5 cm (1-inch) piece of fresh ginger, crushed |
| ¼ teaspoon ground turmeric |
| 1 teaspoon chilli powder or to taste |
| 175 ml (6 fl oz) hot water |

*Serve this as a starter or a snack; it is also ideal for buffets or picnics. If you are entertaining, place the hot chops on a large platter and garnish with slices of beetroot, cucumber slices, sliced hard-boiled eggs, pickled onions, lemon wedges and cress. As mutton chops are not generally available, I have used lamb chops in this recipe.*

Trim off any excess fat from the chops and place them in a heavy pan with a tight-fitting lid. Dry-roast the whole spices, and blend them with the garlic and ginger. To the paste add the turmeric and chilli powder and salt to taste. Add the paste and the hot water to the chops. Mix well and cook the chops slowly until they are

*2 eggs, beaten*

*vegetable oil for deep-frying*

*salt to taste*

tender and all the water has evaporated, 30–35 minutes, with the pan uncovered for the last ten minutes. Dip the cooked chops in the beaten egg and deep-fry them for a few minutes in hot oil until golden brown, turning once. Serve hot with tomato ketchup or garnished as described in the introduction.

# KOTHU ERACHI KARI

Tamil Nadu mince                                    Serves 4–6

Preparation time: 15 minutes + 50 minutes cooking

*2 tablespoons vegetable oil*

*2 onions, chopped finely*

*2 tomatoes, chopped finely*

*10 large dry red chillies, de-seeded if wished*

*1 teaspoon cumin seeds*

*1 tablespoon coriander seeds*

*1 teaspoon poppy seeds*

*2 cloves*

*2.5 cm (1-inch) stick of cinnamon*

*2.5 cm (1-inch) piece of fresh ginger*

*2 cloves of garlic*

*1 tablespoon desiccated coconut*

*500 g (1 lb) minced lamb or beef*

*a little hot water*

*salt to taste*

**To garnish:**

*coriander leaves*

*fried cashew nuts*

*In India, mince is made from mutton as beef is not very popular. I use the lean minced beef or minced lamb for this dish.*

Heat the oil in a large pan or a wok and fry the onions and tomatoes until the onions are soft and translucent. Meanwhile, dry-roast the dry chillies, whole spices, ginger, garlic and coconut and then blend them to a paste. Reduce the heat under the onions, add the spice paste and fry them until the oil separates. Add the minced meat and mix well using a flat spatula to break up any large lumps. Add a little hot water and salt to taste. Cover and cook until the meat is done (about 45–50 minutes) and there is a thick gravy. Garnish with coriander leaves and fried cashew nuts. Serve with rice or Chappatis (page 26) or ordinary bread which has been warmed. If you cook the mixture till it is very dry you can use it as a sandwich filling.

*Kothu Erachi Kari (Tamil Nadu mince)*
*Attu Erachi Chops (Madras-style lamb chops)*

# SEEKH KEBABS

Skewered grilled kebabs                    Serves 4–6 (or more as a snack)

Preparation time: 15 minutes + 1 hour marinating + 25 minutes cooking

| |
|---|
| 500 g (1 lb) lean minced beef |
| 1 large onion, chopped very finely |
| 5 cm (2-inch) piece of fresh ginger, crushed |
| 2 cloves of garlic, crushed |
| 1 teaspoon chilli powder or to taste |
| a few sprigs of fresh coriander, chopped |
| 1 teaspoon garam masala or five-spice powder |
| 2 teaspoons ground coriander |
| 1 teaspoon ground cumin |
| 2 teaspoons ground almonds |
| 1 egg |
| 4 teaspoons gram flour or cornflour |
| a little yogurt and oil |
| salt to taste |

*These are spicy and delicious. The most important ingredient of a perfect kebab, whether skewered or pan-fried, is good meat free of fat and gristle, well marinated and cooked, literally, to a turn.*

In a large bowl mix all the ingredients except the yogurt and oil. Knead well to blend in all the ingredients and allow to marinate for about 1 hour. Grease some skewers. Shape the meat mixture into elongated egg shapes and thread them on to the skewers. Brush with yogurt and oil and grill under a preheated grill for 20–25 minutes. Turn the skewers from time to time and brush them lightly with oil. Remove the skewers and serve hot with onion rings, lemon wedges, salt to taste, and Kirakai Pudina Pacchhadi (Yogurt with cucumber and mint, page 84).

# SEEKH KEBAB SALAN

Skewered grilled kebab curry                                        Serves 4–6

Basic recipe: Seekh Kebabs (above)
Preparation and cooking time: 1 hour 25 minutes + 1 hour marinating

| |
|---|
| 500 g (1 lb) Seekh Kebabs, cooked |
| **For the curry:** |
| 4 tablespoons vegetable oil |
| 1 large onion, sliced finely |
| 2 large tomatoes, chopped |

*After a barbecue party I had some leftover kebabs and had to rejuvenate them, as kebabs are best only when eaten fresh. That is how this recipe came about, but my family enjoyed it so much that I often prepare it without waiting for days when we have leftovers.*

Cut the cooked kebabs into bite-size pieces and keep them aside. Heat the oil in a large pan or a

| | |
|---|---|
| 5 cm (2-inch) piece of fresh ginger, crushed | wok and fry the onion until it is golden brown Reduce the heat and add the tomatoes, ginger and garlic; stir-fry for about 2 minutes. Mix all the ground spices, ground rice and salt to taste with a little water to make a paste. Add this to the onion and stir-fry till the oil separates. Add the kebab pieces and mix well to coat the pieces with the paste. Add the hot water and allow to simmer until the kebabs are well heated, about 20 minutes. Just before taking the pan off the heat, add the coriander leaves and lemon juice. Serve hot with the *Variation* on boiled rice *Bagare Chawal* (page 18) or Chappatis (page 26). |
| 2 cloves of garlic, crushed | |
| 2 teaspoons ground coriander | |
| 1 teaspoon ground cumin | |
| 1 teaspoon ground turmeric | |
| 1 teaspoon chilli powder or to taste | |
| 1 teaspoon garam masala | |
| 1 teaspoon ground rice | |
| 175 ml (6 fl oz) hot water | |

*Note:* If you are trying this recipe with leftover kebabs, add quartered potatoes to the curry to complement the dish and serve with halved hard-boiled eggs. Seekh Kebab Salan should be frozen without potato, and the potatoes added when reheating.

a few fresh coriander leaves, chopped

lemon juice to taste

salt to taste

# PASINDAY

Pan-cooked lamb kebabs (Pictured on page 5)                Serves 4–6

Preparation time: 15 minutes + 2 hours resting +  45 minutes cooking

| | |
|---|---|
| 275 g (9 oz) onions | *Although these are kebabs, they can be cooked very slowly in a pan until there is no gravy, leaving the meat moist and succulent. There are many versions but this recipe, which uses only fresh herbs, is my favourite. Serve these hot as a starter with a tossed salad if you are serving your meal in courses.* |
| 4 cloves of garlic | |
| 5 cm (2-inch) piece of fresh ginger | |
| 1/2 a bunch of coriander leaves and tender stems | |
| 10 green chillies, de-seeded if wished | |

Blend the first five ingredients with salt to taste to a paste in a food processor; use oil if necessary to facilitate this. Rub the paste on to the meat and allow it to stand for 2 hours.

a little vegetable oil (optional)

750 g (1½ lb) boneless lamb, cut in small cubes

4 tablespoons concentrated butter or ghee

salt to taste

Gently heat the concentrated butter or ghee in a heavy pan and add the meat with all the marinade and any juices that have separated. Fry till the meat pieces are of an even colour. Cover and simmer till the meat is tender, about 35 minutes or more, depending on the cut of meat used. If there is excess gravy cook for the last 10 minutes or so uncovered until all the gravy has been absorbed. Serve with lemon wedges.

# SHAMI KEBABS

Minced meat kebabs                Serves 10–12

Preparation time: 15 minutes + 1 hour cooking + 2 hours chilling

275 g (9 oz) boneless leg of lamb, cut into very small pieces

50 g (2 oz) chick-peas or channa dhal

1 teaspoon ground cumin

½ teaspoon garam masala

½ teaspoon chilli powder

1 green chilli, de-seeded if wished

2.5 cm (1-inch) piece of fresh ginger, crushed

a few sprigs of fresh coriander

175 ml (6 fl oz) water

1 teaspoon lemon juice

a little wholemeal or gram flour

2 eggs, beaten

concentrated butter, ghee or oil for shallow-frying

salt to taste

*Appetising and hot, kebabs are ideal for dinner and lunch. Serve them on a large plate attractively garnished with finely shredded lettuce, sliced tomatoes and onion rings accompanied with your favourite chutney and lemon wedges. When I was at school in India I used to pack these into my lunch box, with bread and some salad.*

Put everything except the lemon juice, flour, eggs and ghee or oil in a pan and cook till the meat and chick-peas are tender and there is no water left, about 45 minutes. Remove from the heat and allow to cool. When cool, grind everything to a fine paste in a food processor. To the paste add the lemon juice and mix well. (If your paste is not pliable add a little wholemeal flour or gram flour.) Knead well, divide the paste into 10–12 equal portions, roll into balls and then flatten them out gently. Chill the kebabs for 2 hours to firm them up. Dip the kebabs in the beaten eggs, heat the butter, ghee or oil and shallow-fry them for a couple of minutes on each side until golden brown. Serve hot.

*Attu Erachi Kari (Madras meat curry*

Handi Mamsa Thali (Pork fry)

Shami Kebabs (Minced meat kebabs)

45

# ATTU ERACHI KARI

Madras meat curry                                     Serves 4–6

Preparation time: 15 minutes + 1¾ hours cooking

4 tablespoons vegetable oil

1 large onion, sliced finely

3 cloves

4 green cardamoms, bruised

4 green chillies, or to taste,
de-seeded if wished and
chopped finely

2.5 cm (1-inch) piece of
fresh ginger, crushed

2 cloves of garlic, crushed

2 teaspoons ground coriander

1 teaspoon ground turmeric

2 large dry red chillies,
coarsely broken and
de-seeded if wished

500 g (1 lb) boneless neck
fillet or leg of lamb, cut into
small pieces

a little hot water

4 tablespoons tamarind juice

salt to taste

**To garnish:**

fresh coriander leaves

*In 1962 and 1963 I was a boarder in a convent in
Madras and was allowed out once every six months;
the first thing I always did was go to 'Buhari', a
famous chain of Muslim restaurants, where I always
feasted on this dish with rice as the convent food was
very dull and routine.*

Heat the oil in a heavy pan and fry the onion,
cloves and cardamoms until the onions are
golden brown. Reduce the heat and add the
green chillies, ginger, garlic, coriander,
turmeric and dry chillies. Stir-fry for 2 minutes.
Add the meat and sauté until all the pieces are of
an even colour. Add a little hot water, cover the
pan and simmer until the meat is nearly done
about 1¼ hours. Add the tamarind juice and salt
to taste. Mix well and continue to simmer until
the meat is tender. Garnish with fresh coriander
leaves and serve hot with either plain boiled rice,
Chappatis (page 26) or Poories (page 23).

# HANDI MAMSA THALI

Pork fry                                              Serves 4–6

Preparation time: 15 minutes + 1 hour cooking

1 kg (2 lb) meaty spare ribs,
cut into 7.5 cm (3-inch)
pieces with the bone

*The tradition-bound Coorgs are generally well off:
one sees hardly any poverty amongst them, and this is
very noticeable when they celebrate 'poli poli-deva'
('may everyone have bountiful feast') during*

| | |
|---|---|
| 1–2 teaspoons ground turmeric | |
| 6 green chillies, de-seeded if wished | |
| 10 cloves of garlic | |
| 5 cm (2-inch) piece of fresh ginger | |
| 1 tablespoon cumin seeds | |
| 1 tablespoon black peppercorns | |
| 2 tablespoons coriander seeds | |
| 6 tablespoons vegetable oil | |
| ½ teaspoon mustard seeds | |
| 1 onion, diced | |
| 350 ml (12 fl oz) hot water | |
| ½ teaspoon freshly ground black pepper | |
| 1 tablespoon malt vinegar | |
| 1 tablespoon tomato purée | |
| salt to taste | |

*November and December. With other traditional dishes this is served for the festival meal which ends with fireworks, folk singing and a fancy dress parade.*

Smear the pork pieces with turmeric and salt to taste and keep them aside. Blend the chillies, garlic and ginger to a paste. Dry-roast the cumin seeds, peppercorns, coriander seeds and coarsely grind them. Heat the oil in a large, heavy pan and fry the mustard seeds till they crackle. Add the onion and fry it until it browns. Reduce the heat and add the chilli paste and ground spices and fry for 2 minutes. Add the pork and stir-fry until all the pork pieces are evenly coloured. Add the hot water and bring it to the boil. Then lower the heat and allow it to simmer, covered, until tender, about an hour. When the pork is nearly done add the black pepper, vinegar and tomato purée and stir well. Check the seasoning and simmer uncovered for about 5 minutes, so that the sauce reduces and thickens. Serve hot.

## SUFEED KHURDI

White lamb curry                                           Serves 4–6

Preparation time: 15 minutes + 1¼ hours cooking

| | |
|---|---|
| 1 kg (2 lb) breast of lamb | |
| 5 cm (2-inch) piece of ginger, crushed | |
| 8 cloves of garlic, crushed | |
| 700 ml (1¼ pints) hot water | |
| 2 tablespoons concentrated butter or ghee | |
| 2 teaspoons ground cumin | |
| 5 cm (2-inch) stick of cinnamon | |

*This is only prepared by 'bhoris', a small sect of the Shia Muslims to which I belong. Although 'bhori' dishes are well known in India the secrets of the recipes were jealously guarded, or at least were until I came along. This is a mild dish.*

Trim off as much fat as possible from the lamb and cut it into bite-size pieces. Place the lamb, ginger, garlic and hot water, with salt to taste, in a large pan and bring to the boil. Allow the meat to simmer until it is nearly tender and beginning to come off the bones, about 45 minutes, and then set it aside.

| | |
|---|---|
| 4 cloves | |
| 6 black peppercorns | |
| 3 tablespoons wheat flour or wholemeal flour, sieved | |
| 150 ml (¼ pint) milk | |
| salt to taste | |
| **To garnish:** | |
| fresh coriander and mint leaves | |

In a fresh pan, heat the concentrated butter or ghee gently and fry the cumin, cinnamon, cloves and peppercorns until they are aromatic. Add the flour and stir as for roux sauce until you have a golden-brown colour. Slowly start adding some of the lamb stock and mix well until there are no lumps. Add the remaining stock and the lamb and cook, covered, until the oil rises above the gravy, about 15 minutes. Cool the curry a little, fold in the milk and mix well and bring it to the boil again. Serve hot, garnished with coriander and mint leaves with any bread you like. Do not freeze.

## ATTIARICHI KARI

Kerala meat curry                    Serves 4–6

Preparation time: 20 minutes + 1 hour marinating + 1 hour cooking

500 g (1 lb) boneless shoulder or leg of lamb, cut into bite-size pieces

1 teaspoon ground turmeric

1 teaspoon chilli powder

350 ml (12 fl oz) water

12–14 black peppercorns

5 cm (2-inch) stick of cinnamon

25 g (1 oz) creamed coconut

4 tablespoons vegetable oil

1 large onion, sliced finely

2 dry red chillies, de-seeded if wished

2 teaspoons coriander seeds

5 cloves

4 tablespoons tamarind juice

salt to taste

1 teaspoon aniseed, dry-roasted and ground

*My in-laws in Kerala prepared this dish when I visited them and I was told that the recipe had been handed down by word of mouth for four generations.*

Rub the meat with the turmeric and chilli powder and salt to taste and set it aside for one hour. Simmer the meat in the water for 20 minutes along with 6–8 of the peppercorns and half the cinnamon stick. Drain and reserve the stock, discarding the peppercorns and cinnamon if you wish. To half the reserved stock add the creamed coconut and allow it to dissolve. Heat the oil and fry the sliced onion in a heavy pan until browned. Meanwhile, dry-roast the dry chillies, coriander seeds, cloves, remaining peppercorns and the other half of the cinnamon stick and then grind them to a fine paste. Reduce the heat under the onion, add the ground ingredients and fry for 1 minute. Add the meat and the stock and cook till the meat is tender, a further 40 minutes. Add the coconut mixture and tamarind juice and bring to the boil. Serve hot, sprinkling on the ground aniseed as a garnish.

# SEAFOOD DISHES

The south of India has luxurious coastlines and boasts lush and languorous beach resorts. When touring south India in 1984 with an English friend we took four days off to relax at Mahabalipuram, the temple town near Madras. Each morning while taking breakfast we watched the fishing fleet coming in and before we left the dining room we were asked to choose our supper from the day's haul. A mark was placed on what we chose – a lobster, crab, giant prawns, fresh pomfrets (a fish like plaice) and so on – and then we awaited the evenings to savour the cuisine of the area while lapping up the sunshine and sipping fresh coconut milk.

## MACCHLI MUSSALAM

| Muslim-style fish | Serves 4–6 |
| --- | --- |

Preparation time: 40 minutes + 1 hour marinating

| |
| --- |
| 1 kg (2 lb) cod cutlets with bone |
| 500 g (1 lb) carton of natural yogurt, beaten |
| 2 onions, sliced finely |
| 5 cloves of garlic |
| 5 cm (2-inch) piece of fresh ginger |
| 4 green chillies, de-seeded if wished |
| 2 tablespoons sesame oil |
| 2 tablespoons vegetable oil |
| 1 teaspoon fenugreek seeds |
| 1 tablespoon cornflour or gram flour if necessary |
| a little hot water if necessary |
| salt to taste |

*Although Hyderabad is on the Deccan Plateau, sufficient fish is available from local fish farms. In my home in India fish is only cooked on the days my senior aunt is away, as she is allergic to seafood. Every piece of equipment and the whole kitchen has to be sterilised before her return, but we all love fish and particularly this dish, so its worth all the trouble.*

Marinade the fish with the yogurt and salt to taste for an hour or more. Blend one of the sliced onions with the garlic, ginger and green chillies in a food processor and keep aside. Heat the oils in a wok or a large frying pan and fry the fenugreek seeds until they swell. Add the remaining sliced onion and fry until it is golden-brown in colour. Add the ground paste and fry till the raw smell disappears. Reduce the heat and carefully add the fish, with the yogurt; add a tablespoon of cornflour or gram flour if necessary to stop the yogurt curdling. Gently stir and after

a few minutes turn the fish over. Sprinkle on a
little hot water if necessary, cover the wok or
pan and cook gently until the fish is done, about
20 minutes. Garnish with the deep-fried onions
and serve hot. Do not freeze.

## MURREL KARI

Special mackerel curry                    Serves 4–6

Preparation time: 45 minutes + 35 minutes cooking

750 g (1½ lb) mackerel

1½ onions

5 tablespoons vegetable oil

6 tablespoons desiccated
coconut

4 dry red chillies, de-seeded
if wished

8 black peppercorns

2 tablespoons rice

½ tablespoon mustard seeds

1 teaspoon gram flour

75 ml (3 fl oz) tamarind
juice

1 teaspoon ground turmeric

175 ml (6 fl oz) hot water

salt to taste

*At Kanniyakumari (Cape Comorin), the southern-
most point of India where we broke our journey
between Trivandrum and Madurai, this was the dish
we selected before setting off to experience the sunset
and the moonrise simultaneously: this wonderful
incident occurs with the full moon.*

Clean and trim the fish and cut each into four
pieces, keeping the heads (as Indians do) or
discarding them. Rub the fish with some salt and
wash them thoroughly. Leave to drain in a
colander.

Slice half an onion and in a large frying pan or
a wok heat three tablespoons of oil and gently
fry the sliced onion, desiccated coconut, chillies,
peppercorns, rice and mustard seeds for about
5 minutes. Remove and allow to cool. Place all
the fried ingredients with the frying oil in a food
processor and blend them to a paste. Mix in the
gram flour. Dice the remaining onion, heat the
remaining oil in the same pan or wok and fry the
diced onion until brown. Add the ground paste,
tamarind juice, turmeric and salt to taste. Bring
everything to the boil and then add the hot
water. Bring to the boil again and allow to
simmer until the vinegar smell from the
tamarind begins to disappear; add the fish pieces.
Cover the fish pieces with the gravy, cover the
pan and allow it to simmer gently until the fish is
done, about 20 minutes. Stir once or twice but
be careful not to break up the fish pieces. Serve
hot with rice.

# NANDU KARI

Madras crab curry                                          Serves 4–6

Preparation time: 1 hour + 15 minutes cooking

| |
|---|
| 6 medium-size crabs |
| 4 tablespoons vegetable oil |
| 1 large onion, sliced finely |
| 6 cloves of garlic, sliced finely |
| 2.5 cm (1-inch) piece of fresh ginger, sliced finely |
| 1 large tomato, chopped |
| 6 green chillies, or more to taste, de-seeded if wished and chopped |
| 6 tablespoons desiccated coconut |
| 1 teaspoon aniseed |
| 1 teaspoon poppy seeds |
| 10 blanched almonds |
| 1 teaspoon garam masala |
| 1 teaspoon ground coriander |
| ½ teaspoon chilli powder |
| 2.5 cm (1-inch) stick of cinnamon |
| 3 green cardamoms, bruised |
| 175 ml (6 fl oz) hot water |
| salt to taste |

**To garnish:**

coriander leaves and lemon wedges (optional)

*Crab curry is a favourite dish around the entire coast of south India, with each region making their own variation. This recipe comes from outside Madras where at Mahabalipuram (the village of shore temples) I spent the last four days of my trip. The beaches, pleasant people and delicious seafood made me relax after the hustle and bustle of the previous nine weeks and in fact made me feel I was on a different planet altogether.*

Remove the large crab shells and discard any fibrous tissues found under the shell. Divide each body into four. Break the large claws and crack them with a hammer to make them easier to eat. Separate the smaller claws and leave them whole.

Heat the oil and fry the onion, garlic, ginger, tomato and green chillies until the onions are translucent. Remove them from the oil, blend them in a food processor and keep them aside. Dry-roast the coconut, aniseed, poppy seeds and almonds and grind them to a smooth paste. Mix in the garam masala, ground coriander powder and chilli powder and keep aside.

Reheat the oil in a large pan or wok and fry the cinnamon and cardamoms until they are aromatic. Add the onion and spice pastes and stir-fry for 2 minutes. Add the crab meat and claws and mix well. Add the hot water and simmer for about 15 minutes or till the meat is cooked. Garnish if wished and serve hot.

*Alternatives:* Use 500 g (1 lb) fresh crab meat. Follow the same method but decrease the water to 150 ml (¼ pint) and allow to simmer for 7–10 minutes only. Or use 500 g (1 lb) frozen crab meat. Allow it to thaw completely and drain off any excess water. Proceed as for fresh crab meat.

# CHEMMEEN KARI

Kerala prawn curry

Serves 4–6

Preparation time: 35 minutes

|  |
|---|
| 500 g (1 lb) large raw or cooked prawns |
| 4 teaspoons malt vinegar |
| 4 large dry red chillies |
| 6 tablespoons desiccated coconut |
| 1 teaspoon mustard seeds |
| 1 large onion, sliced |
| 4 tablespoons vegetable oil |
| 10 curry leaves |
| 5 cm (2-inch) piece of fresh ginger, crushed |
| 2 cloves of garlic, crushed |
| 1 teaspoon ground turmeric |
| 1 tablespoon ground coriander |
| 1 teaspoon chilli powder (optional) |
| 2 large tomatoes, chopped |
| 125 ml (4 fl oz) hot water |
| salt to taste |

**To garnish:**

coriander leaves (optional)

*At Alleppey, a coastal town in Kerala, my husband's family have been fishing for generations. This is my grandmother-in-law's recipe, the secret of which she disclosed on my last visit.*

Shell the prawns and de-vein them by lightly slitting the back. Rub them with a little salt and two teaspoons of vinegar and keep aside. Dry-roast the chillies, coconut, mustard seeds and onion and then blend them to a fine paste to make a *masala*. Heat the oil in a wok or a large pan and fry the curry leaves for 1 minute. Reduce the heat and add the ginger and garlic and fry for a few minutes until the raw smell disappears. Add the turmeric, ground coriander and chilli powder and the masala. Stir-fry until the oil separates. Add the tomatoes, salt to taste and the hot water. Bring to the boil and then allow them to simmer for 5 minutes. Drain the prawns, add them to the gravy and mix well. The cooking time now depends on the size of the prawns: very large prawns take about ten minutes. As they begin to cook they will start to curl and turn a pinky-orange colour. Add the remaining vinegar and cook for a further two minutes. Do not cook the prawns too long, whatever their size, as they tend to shrivel and become hard and dry. Garnish with the coriander leaves if wished and serve hot.

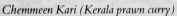

*Chemmeen Kari (Kerala prawn curry)*

*Murrel Kari (Special mackerel curry)*

*Nandu Kari
(Madras crab curry)*

53

# CHEMMEEN ACHAR

Pickled prawns                                    Makes three 250 g (8 oz) jars

Preparation time: 30 minutes + 30 minutes resting

*1 kg (2 lb) large raw or cooked prawns, shelled*

*1 teaspoon ground turmeric*

*300 ml (½ pint) mustard oil or vegetable oil*

*2 teaspoons ground asafoetida*

*10–15 curry leaves*

*1 teaspoon mustard seeds*

*25 cloves of garlic, crushed*

*4 teaspoons ground coriander*

*4 teaspoons chilli powder*

*10 green chillies, slit lengthways and de-seeded if wished*

*juice of 8 lemons or 125 ml (4 fl oz) malt vinegar*

*salt to taste*

*My last visit to India was during the monsoons. My uncle-in-law took me out fishing one day and from our haul of giant-sized prawns my aunt made this pickle, which travelled with me for the remaining twenty-one days of my tour and made a delicious accompaniment to any meal.*

De-vein the prawns by lightly slitting the backs. Rub them with turmeric and a little salt and allow them to stand for 30 minutes. Heat the oil in a wok or a large pan and when it is nearly smoking reduce the heat and add the asafoetida, curry leaves and mustard seeds (if you are using mustard oil ensure you have a window open as it stings the eyes). When the mustard seeds begin to crackle add the garlic, ground coriander, chilli powder and green chillies and gently fry them on a reduced heat. Continue frying until the raw garlic smell disappears. Add the lemon juice or vinegar and salt to taste and bring it to the boil. Reduce the heat again and add the drained prawns. Mix well and cook until the prawns are done (they should curl up and turn a pinky-orange colour). Cool thoroughly and bottle in sterilised jars. It will keep for up to 3 months.

If you wish you can serve this as a curry, in which case reduce the oil to 6 tablespoons but prepare it 24 hours before serving and when reheating do it quickly to prevent the prawns from becoming dry and hard.

*Note:* If raw prawns are difficult to come by use the largest cooked prawns you can buy. When you have added the vinegar allow the mixture to simmer for a little longer and when you have added the cooked prawns cook them only for 5 minutes.

If you wish to reheat the pickle before serving, do it quickly and only reheat the portion required. This recipe is suitable for freezing, and also for simply storing as long as there is oil floating above the pickle.

# MACCHLI AUR BHENDI

Fish curry with okra                                          Serves 4–6

Preparation time: 55 minutes

500 g (1 lb) fish without bones (use halibut, cod, coley or monkfish)

1½ teaspoons ground turmeric

½ teaspoon chilli powder

½ teaspoon salt, plus extra to taste

oil for shallow-frying

1 onion, chopped finely

1 teaspoon cumin seeds

½ teaspoon fennel seeds

¼ teaspoon fenugreek seeds

12 dry red chillies

5 cloves of garlic

2.5 cm (1-inch) piece of fresh ginger

a pinch of sugar

a little malt vinegar (optional)

2 large tomatoes, skinned and chopped finely

a little hot water

250 g (8 oz) okra, tops sparingly trimmed

salt to taste

**To garnish:**

a handful of fresh coriander leaves

*This was invented in my kitchen, but as I am a south Indian by birth it bears a certain similarity to a Deccani curry. It is a hot dish, so adjust it to suit your taste. Delicious with rice and Koshumbri (Green gram salad, page 62).*

Cut the fish into small pieces and dry them well. Mix the turmeric, chilli powder and ½ teaspoon salt and rub the mixture on to the pieces of fish. Heat enough oil for shallow-frying in a non-stick wok or a large frying-pan which has a lid. When the oil is nearly smoking fry the pieces of fish until they are golden brown on all sides. Drain the fish and keep it warm. Heat the oil again and fry the onion until brown. Meanwhile, dry-roast the cumin, fennel and fenugreek seeds and then blend them to a paste with the chillies, garlic, ginger and a pinch of sugar; add a little vinegar, if necessary, to facilitate the blending. Reduce the heat under the pan and add the paste. Fry until the raw smell disappears and the oil separates. Add the tomatoes, salt to taste and a little hot water and fry gently till the tomatoes have blended into the gravy. Add the okra and fried fish pieces and mix gently, coating the fish and okra with the gravy. Cover the wok or frying pan and gently simmer for about 10 minutes, stirring once or twice without breaking the fish pieces. Serve hot, garnished with coriander leaves. Do not freeze.

# BHARI HUVEY MACCHLI

Stuffed fish                                          Serves 4–6

Preparation time: 20 minutes + 10 minutes frying or 20 minutes baking

*4 medium-size Dover or
lemon sole or pomfrets*

*a little malt vinegar*

*4 tablespoons desiccated
coconut*

*a bunch of coriander leaves*

*4 green chillies, de-seeded if
wished*

*4 cloves of garlic*

*1 teaspoon sugar*

*juice of 2 lemons (optional)*

*2 firm tomatoes, sliced*

*2 hard-boiled eggs, sliced*

*oil for deep-frying or
greasing*

*salt to taste*

**Oven temperature:**
*Gas Mark 4/180°C/350°F*

*After visiting relatives in Alleppey we took a boat trip
through the backwaters to Quilon where I have
Anglo-Indian friends whom I had not seen for over
twenty years. We arrived on a Friday and it was
inevitable we would be served fish, as Catholics there
still abide by the ancient law. This dish can be deep-
fried or baked. When cooked, the fish can either be
served whole, accompanied by Dadhyodhana (Curd
rice, page 22) and stir-fried vegetables, or cut into
thick slices and served with boiled rice and a lentil
curry.*

Preheat the oven if the dish is to be baked. Trim
and clean the fish and rub them inside and outside
with a little vinegar and salt. Keep aside. In a
food processor blend the desiccated coconut,
coriander leaves, chillies, garlic and sugar, using
the lemon juice if necessary to facilitate
grinding. Wipe the fish lightly with a kitchen
towel and stuff them with equal portions of the
ground paste. Season them and then arrange the
slices of tomatoes and egg over the ground paste
inside the fish.

To cook the fish, either tie them two or three
times with white cotton to keep them closed and
deep-fry them in hot vegetable oil for about 10
minutes, or bake them in a greased baking dish
covered with foil for 20–25 minutes.

When serving a whole fish, ask the diners to
eat the flesh from the top side of the fish first and
remove the whole bone and then to eat the
bottom half. In the east it is considered unlucky
to turn the fish over as it represents a boat and if
you turn it over it signifies a drowning.

*Bhari Huvey Macchli (Stuffed fish)*

# MEEN MOOLEE

Kerala fish in coconut milk　　　　　　　　　　　Serves 4–6

Preparation time: 15 minutes + 35 minutes cooking

*500 g (1 lb) firm white fish, cut in large pieces*

*4 tablespoons vegetable oil*

*1 large onion, sliced finely*

*5 cloves of garlic, sliced finely*

*2.5 cm (1-inch) piece of fresh ginger, sliced finely*

*5 green chillies, de-seeded if wished and chopped finely*

*1 teaspoon ground turmeric*

*3 medium-size potatoes, peeled and cubed*

*175 ml (6 fl oz) thin coconut milk (see page 12)*

*75 ml (3 fl oz) thick coconut milk (see page 12)*

*3 teaspoons malt vinegar*

*salt to taste*

**To garnish:**

*chopped coriander*

*Moolee is a popular variation of curry in the south and the coconut milk makes it deliciously mild. It could be considered as a lovely stew. If you have enjoyed Chemmeen Kari (Kerala prawn curry, page 52) try this also with large raw prawns or use a fish like halibut, cod, mullet, monkfish or plaice.*

Rub the fish pieces with some salt and leave them aside. Heat the oil in a wok or a large pan and fry the onion, garlic, ginger and green chillies until the onion is golden-brown. Reduce the heat and add the turmeric, potatoes and salt to taste. Mix well to coat the potato pieces evenly. Add the thin coconut milk and allow the potato to simmer until nearly cooked, about 10 minutes. Drain the fish and add the pieces to the pan. Carefully cover the fish with the gravy and continue to simmer gently until nearly cooked, a further 10 minutes, stirring gently to prevent the fish pieces breaking up. Finally, add the thick coconut milk and vinegar and bring it to a quick boil without covering the pan. Garnish with coriander and serve hot with boiled rice or bread. Do not freeze.

# TALI MEEN

Fish fry　　　　　　　　　　　　　　　　　　　Serves 4–6

Preparation time: 30 minutes + 30 minutes resting

*500 g (1 lb) white fish, cut in bite-size pieces*

*½ teaspoon cumin seeds*

*1 teaspoon aniseed*

*12 dry red chillies, de-seeded if wished*

*Practically all non-vegetarian families who live along the coasts of south India prepare this dish on a daily basis. Use any firm fish, such as cod, haddock or monkfish, or try the famous pomfret, a flat fish like a sole with an earthy flavour.*

To give flavour, rub the fish pieces with some

4 cloves of garlic

vegetable oil for deep-frying

salt to taste

salt, rinse, drain well and leave in a colander. Blend the spices with the garlic and salt to taste to a smooth paste. Dry the fish. Smear the fish with the ground mixture and leave it for 30 minutes.

Heat the oil in a wok or a large frying pan and when it is nearly smoking add the pieces of fish and deep-fry until they are golden brown and slightly crisp on all sides, about 15 minutes. Do not overcrowd the pan and use a slotted spoon or wooden- or metal-tipped chopsticks for turning. Serve the fish with lemon wedges, boiled rice and a lentil dish.

## FARMAISHI MACCHLI

Fish request                                                    Serves 4–6

Preparation time: 40 minutes + 30 minutes marinating

750 g (1½ lb) fillets of any firm white fish

juice of 2 lemons

2 cloves

3 green cardamoms, peeled

6–8 black peppercorns

2.5 cm (1-inch) piece of fresh ginger

a bunch of coriander leaves

4 tablespoons vegetable oil

a little hot water

a pinch each of ground nutmeg and mace

a few strands of saffron, soaked in a little warm water

2 large onions, sliced and deep-fried until brown and crisp

salt to taste

chopped coriander

*This is the way my father often requested his fish curry and therefore I have given it this name. He would often instruct the cook how certain dishes should be prepared.*

Cut the fish into bite-size pieces and rub them with a little salt and half the lemon juice. Allow to marinade for about 30 minutes.

Meanwhile, dry-roast the cloves, cardamoms, peppercorns, ginger and coriander leaves and then blend them to a masala. Heat the oil in a wok or large pan and fry the masala until fragrant. Add the fish pieces and stir gently to cover the fish evenly with spices. Add the remaining lemon juice and a few drops of hot water. Cover the pan and allow the fish to cook, turning the pieces over once very gently. After about 20 minutes when the water has dried up and just a thick masala remains with the oil, add the nutmeg, mace and saffron. Add salt to taste. Crush the browned onions and add them to the fish. Stir well but carefully and simmer for a further five minutes. Serve hot, sprinkled with chopped coriander

# LENTIL DISHES

Lentils that have been husked and split are called dhals. In south India, whether you are a vegetarian or a non-vegetarian no day goes by when some form of dhal is not cooked. Moong dhal (green gram), urad dhal (black gram), channa dhal (split peas), tuvar or arhar dhal (red gram) and others like lobia (cow gram), masoor (red lentils) are a few mentioned to give one an idea of the range available in India.

The 'final-fry' (see page 10) of whole spices and oil is added to most dhals in the last stages of cooking and this gives the dhal added zest. This procedure involves fast work and steady hands as the contact of hot oil and spices with the dhal creates a mild explosion which is one of the delights of south Indian cooking. Dhals have been auspicious ingredients since Vedic times and every occasion calls for them, be it sad, joyous or religious. Dhals are very versatile (or maybe we Indians are) for we make them into savoury dishes, soups, rice dishes (kitchdi) and also make sweets like the south Indian favourite Mysore Pak (Gram flour sweet, page 88).

## USILI

| Cluster beans in lentil sauce | Serves 4–6 |
|---|---|

Preparation time: 20 minutes + 30 minutes soaking + 25 minutes cooking

350 g (12 oz) cluster beans or whole green beans

125 g (4 oz) red lentils

4 dry red chillies

a pinch of ground asafoetida

4 tablespoons vegetable oil

1 teaspoon mustard seeds

lemon juice to taste

salt to taste

*Cluster beans or gypsy beans (guvar) are a popular vegetable all over India. They have a very slightly bitter taste and when you chew one or two raw beans they cleanse the teeth and are very refreshing.*

Wash and string the beans and cut them into 2.5 cm (1-inch) pieces. Blanch them in boiling water for 3 minutes and then drain them and keep aside, reserving the water. Cool the water and soak the red lentils in it for 30 minutes.

*Koshumbri (Green gram salad)*
*Usili (Cluster beans in lentil sauce)*

Drain the lentils thoroughly, reserving the water, and blend them with the chillies and asafoetida to a coarse paste in a food processor (try to avoid using any liquid, but if absolutely necessary use some of the reserved water, sparingly).

Heat the oil in a large pan or wok and fry the mustard seeds until they crackle. Lower the heat and add the paste. Fry for 2 or 3 minutes. Add the beans, 125 ml (4 fl oz) reserved water and salt to taste. Stir well and allow to cook on a low heat until the beans are done, about 25 minutes. Serve hot, with lemon juice to flavour.

# KOSHUMBRI

Green gram (mung bean) salad                    Serves 4–6

Preparation time: 20 minutes + 30 minutes soaking
+ 12–24 hours germination

*175 g (6 oz) split mung beans (moong dhal)*

*2 green chillies, de-seeded if wished and chopped finely*

*2.5 cm (1-inch) piece of fresh ginger, grated or crushed*

*25 g (1 oz) freshly grated coconut or desiccated coconut, soaked in a little warm water to soften*

*2 tablespoons vegetable oil*

*1/2 teaspoon mustard seeds*

*a pinch of ground asafoetida*

*6 curry leaves, chopped*

*juice of 1 lemon*

*salt to taste*

*A popular salad from Tamil Nadu. As the gram in this salad are germinated they are rich in maltose and dextrose and this makes digestion very easy. Varieties of salads known as Koshumbri and Kosumalli are always included in south Indian meals.*

Wash the mung beans, soak them for 30 minutes and then drain them. Wrap the beans in a wet cloth and cover them till they germinate, usually between 12 and 24 hours but germination time will depend on how warm the atmosphere is.

When the beans have germinated, rinse them under running water and drain well. Place them in a serving bowl and mix in the chillies, ginger and coconut. Heat the oil in a small frying pan and add the mustard seeds, asafoetida and curry leaves and fry till the mustard seeds begin to crackle. Add the oil and the spices to the beans. Add salt to taste and lemon juice and toss well. Chill and serve with any meal. Do not freeze.

*Note:* Grated carrot or cucumber or raw mango can be added to this, with coriander leaves as a garnish.

# SAADI DHAL

Basic lentil curry                                    Serves 4–6

Preparation time: 10 minutes + 40 minutes cooking

175 g (6 oz) red lentils,
picked and washed

1.5 litres (2½ pints) water

½ teaspoon ground turmeric

2 whole green chillies,
de-seeded if wished

1 onion, sliced

a few coriander leaves

salt to taste

**For the 'final-fry':**

4 tablespoons vegetable oil

½ teaspoon mustard seeds

½ teaspoon cumin seeds

1 clove of garlic, crushed

6 curry leaves

2 whole dry red chillies

**To garnish:**

sliced onions, deep-fried
until brown and crisp

*Dhal in one form or another is a daily must in India. This has been our tradition for centuries, for dhal is considered auspicious as well as being high in protein. India is blessed with over a dozen varieties of lentils so lentil dishes need never be repetitive.*

Place the lentils, 1.5 litres (2½ pints) water, turmeric, chillies, onion and coriander leaves in a heavy pan and bring everything to the boil. Then allow it to simmer, covered, until the lentils are nearly mushy, about 30 minutes. (Remember lentils boil over, so keep a watch on the pan.) Drain the water. Mash the lentil mixture with a potato masher until smooth. Heat the remaining water and add it, with salt to taste. Bring to the boil and leave to simmer. While the lentils are simmering, heat the oil in a small frying pan and fry the seasoning ingredients until the mustard seeds begin to crackle. Standing well back, hold the lid of the lentil pan in one hand and with the other pour the oil and the seasoning ingredients over the lentil curry. Cover the lentil pan immediately to retain the aroma. After 5 minutes, mix well. Reheat if necessary and garnish with deep-fried onions; serve hot with plain boiled rice.

# SAMBHAR

Lentil curry with vegetables                                                     Serves 4–6

Preparation time: 20 minutes + 40 minutes cooking

250 g (8 oz) red lentils, picked and washed

2 teaspoons sambhar powder

½ teaspoon ground turmeric

500 ml (18 fl oz) water

8 okra, sparingly trimmed

250 g (8 oz) cauliflower florets

250 g (8 oz) mooli (white radish) peeled and sliced into 2.5 cm (1-inch) pieces

1 onion, sliced thickly

2 tablespoons tamarind juice

1 teaspoon soft brown sugar

4 tomatoes, quartered

1 green or red pepper, cut into large pieces

**For the 'final-fry':**

4 tablespoons vegetable oil

½ teaspoon mustard seeds

2 whole dry red chillies

½ teaspoon cumin seeds

a pinch of ground asafoetida

6 curry leaves

2 cloves of garlic, crushed

salt to taste

**To garnish:**

sliced onions, deep-fried until brown and crisp

coriander leaves

*There are many variations of this but one form or the other is cooked daily in every south Indian home. It can be served with plain rice, Dosais (page 18) or Idlis (page 24). The choice of suitable vegetables is wide; you can combine in similar quantities aubergines, beans, potatoes, kohlrabi, courgettes, marrows, pumpkin, carrots, peppers and turnips.*

Place the lentils, sambhar powder, turmeric and water in a large, heavy pan and bring it to the boil. Lower the heat and cover the pan. Allow to simmer until the lentils are soft and mushy and most of the water has evaporated, about 20 minutes. (Keep a watch as it tends to froth over, in which case leave the pan slightly uncovered.)

When the lentils are soft, mash them with the back of a wooden spoon or a potato masher. Add the okra, cauliflower, mooli, onion, tamarind juice, sugar and salt to taste. Mix well and add enough water to make the consistency of a thick soup. Simmer until the vegetables are done, a further 10 minutes. Add the tomatoes and pepper and mix well. Keep warm.

In a small frying pan, heat the oil and fry the seasoning ingredients until the mustard seeds begin to crackle and the chillies turn dark in colour. Standing well back, pour the oil with the spices over the curry and immediately cover the pan to retain the aroma. Just before serving reheat if necessary and garnish with browned onions and coriander leaves.

*Note:* If you are preparing this dish in advance you may need to adjust the consistency before you serve it, as all lentils when cooked tend to absorb liquid and become thicker. Boiled lentils can be frozen, but the other vegetables should be added later.

*Sambhar (Lentil curry with vegetables)*
*Sookhi Moong Dhal (Dry green gram)*

# SOOKHI MOONG DHAL

Dry green gram                                    Serves 4–6

Preparation time: 40 minutes

175 g (6 oz) split mung
beans (moong dhal)

½ teaspoon ground turmeric

350 ml (12 fl oz) water

4 tablespoons vegetable oil

1 large onion, sliced finely

2 cloves of garlic, crushed

2 whole dry red chillies

½ teaspoon mustard seeds

½ teaspoon cumin seeds

1 teaspoon ground coriander

a pinch of asafoetida

a few coriander leaves

6 curry leaves

a pinch of sugar

2 courgettes, cut into small
pieces

2 firm tomatoes, cut into
small pieces

salt to taste

*I am very partial to this lentil dish, and this recipe is
a highlighted variation which blends in courgettes.
This is my own invention; the first time I prepared it
I promised my sons they would love it and now it is
requested at least once a week.*

In a heavy pan cook the mung beans and
turmeric with the water until tender but not
mushy, about 10–15 minutes. When the beans
are cooked, if there is excess water drain it and
keep both aside. In a wok or a large frying pan
heat the oil and fry the onion until golden
brown. Reduce the heat and add the remaining
ingredients except the courgettes and tomatoes.
Stir-fry for 2–3 minutes. Fold in the courgettes
and add some of the reserved water if necessary.
Cover and allow to cook on a low heat until the
courgettes are done; I cook them for only about
5 minutes, as I do not like my vegetables
overdone. Fold in the tomatoes and the reserved
beans. Mix well and heat through thoroughly.
Serve hot.

   *Note:* This, like all other dry curries, makes an
excellent sandwich filling.

# DECCANI DALCHA

Lentils cooked with meat                                    Serves 4–6

Preparation time: 15 minutes + 2 hours cooking

*225 g (7 oz) chick-peas or split peas*

*750 ml (1¼ pints) water*

*4 tablespoons vegetable oil*

*1 large onion, chopped finely*

*5 cm (2-inch) piece of fresh ginger, crushed*

*2 cloves of garlic, crushed*

*1 teaspoon ground coriander*

*½ teaspoon ground turmeric*

*1 teaspoon chilli powder*

*½ teaspoon ground cumin*

*1 kg (2 lb) shoulder of lamb cut into pieces with bone, or 1 kg (2 lb) lamb chops with bone*

*4 ripe tomatoes, chopped*

*5 green chillies, de-seeded if wished and chopped*

*8 curry leaves*

*a handful of coriander leaves, chopped*

*1 kg (2 lb) bottle gourd, peeled and pith removed, or use marrow or courgettes*

*1 teaspoon garam masala*

*salt to taste*

*Dalcha is prepared by most communities in India, but only the Deccanis excel in it. In 1947, when India was being divided, we stayed on with a Hindu family. They allocated my mother a room where she could cook non-vegetarian meals. Dalcha seemed to be on the menu constantly; perhaps it was to make ends meet while satisfying my father that meat was included.*

In a heavy pan, cook the chick-peas or split peas with the water until tender and mushy, about 1 hour, depending on the peas. Drain any excess water and keep it aside. Mash the chick-peas or split peas until smooth and keep them aside.

In a separate pan, heat the oil and fry the onion until soft. Reduce the heat and add the ginger and garlic, ground spices and salt to taste. Sprinkle on a few drops of the reserved cooking liquid and fry for 2 minutes. Add the meat and fry for a further 5 minutes. Add the tomatoes, green chillies, curry leaves, coriander leaves and remaining cooking liquid. When the meat is tender, after about 30 minutes, cut the bottle gourd, courgettes or marrow into large pieces and add them to the pan with the mashed chick-peas. Simmer till the gourd is soft and the oil floats on top, a further 20 minutes. Sprinkle with the garam masala and serve hot with *Bagare Chawal* (the *Variation* on page 18). Deccani Dalcha may be frozen, but before the bottle gourd is added.

# VEGETABLES

In my opinion no other country offers the range of vegetables that India does. The Hindus in south India are predominantly vegetarians and I have chosen a few of their classic dishes like Kuttu (Mixed vegetables, page 70) from Tamil Nadu and Aviyal (Mixed vegetables in yogurt, page 74), a Malabar masterpiece from the state of Kerala. But the non–vegetarians also excel in vegetable dishes like the long-standing favourite Bagare Baingan (Richly spiced aubergines, page 71) prepared by the Muslims in Hyderabad.

The secret of good vegetarian dishes is to know the art of blending spices and cooking the vegetables to the texture each dish calls for. The recipes in this section have been handed down through generations for centuries.

## GUCCI KARI

| Mushroom curry | Serves 4–6 |
| --- | --- |

Preparation time: 30 minutes

| | |
| --- | --- |
| 2 green chillies, de-seeded if wished | *At Mercara, the capital of Coorg in the state of Karnataka, I boldly invited myself to a wedding lunch. Amongst several other dishes I found this mushroom curry. One noteworthy custom at wedding feasts is that the food is served by lovely young unmarried girls who gracefully make sure the guests are well fed.* |
| 1 teaspoon ground coriander | |
| 1 teaspoon ground cumin | |
| 1 teaspoon chilli powder | |
| 4 cloves of garlic | |
| 1 small onion | |
| 500 g (1 lb) small button mushrooms | Blend the chillies, ground spices, garlic and onion to a paste with salt to taste. Wash and trim the mushrooms if necessary. Place the thin coconut milk and ground ingredients in a pan and bring them to the boil. Reduce the heat and add the mushrooms (saving a few for garnish). Cook till the mushrooms are nearly done, about 20 minutes. Add the thick coconut milk and cook uncovered until the gravy is thick. Remove from the heat. While the curry is cooking, |
| 175 ml (6 fl oz) thin coconut milk (page 12) | |
| 125 ml (4 fl oz) thick coconut milk (page 12) | |
| a little butter or vegetable oil | |
| salt to taste | |

prepare the reserved mushrooms for garnish by sautéing them in a little butter or oil. Serve the curry garnished with the sautéed mushrooms and wedges of tomato. Do not freeze.

## TAMATAR KA CUT

Tomato curry (Pictured on page 4)                    Serves 4–6

Preparation time: 1 hour

500 g (1 lb) ripe red tomatoes

2 tablespoons desiccated coconut, browned

2 teaspoons coriander seeds

2 teaspoons poppy seeds

2 teaspoons sesame seeds

a little vegetable oil

2 teaspoons gram flour

2.5 cm (1-inch) piece of fresh ginger, crushed

4 cloves of garlic, crushed

1 teaspoon chilli powder

350 ml (12 fl oz) water

salt to taste

**For the 'final-fry':**

1 tablespoon sesame oil

1 tablespoon vegetable oil

1 teaspoon cumin seeds

4 whole dry red chillies

6 curry leaves

4 cloves of garlic, crushed

a pinch of ground asafoetida

*Another very Muslim dish. When prepared in India it is served with biryani or any pilau. I have reduced the chilli quantity; when this is prepared in Hyderabad the colour of the final dish is bright red not just from the tomatoes but because of the red chillies. Increase the chillies gradually to suit your taste. Because this dish is so hot it is eaten in small quantities.*

Wash and chop the tomatoes and place them in a large, heavy pan. Dry-roast the coconut, coriander, poppy and sesame seeds and then grind them to a paste using a little oil to facilitate grinding. Add the paste, gram flour, ginger, garlic, chilli powder, salt and water to the tomatoes. Bring to the boil and then cover the pan and allow to simmer until the tomatoes are pulpy, about 15 minutes. Remove from the heat and pass the mixture through a sieve, discarding any seeds and peel. Return the sieved tomato juice to the pan and simmer until it reaches the consistency of tomato soup, about 20 minutes.

Heat the oils in a small frying pan and when they are nearly smoking, fry the cumin seeds, red chillies, curry leaves, garlic and asafoetida until the red chillies are nearly black in colour. Pour the oil and spices over the tomato curry and cover the pan immediately to retain the aroma. Reheat well before serving.

*Note:* To highlight the curry, float halved hard-boiled eggs on the surface and sprinkle on a few chopped coriander leaves. This freezes well, but add the eggs just before you serve it.

# KUTTU

Tamil Nadu mixed vegetables                    Serves 4–6

Preparation time: 45 minutes

*125 g (4 oz) red lentils, picked, washed and drained*

*750 ml (1¼ pints) water*

*½ teaspoon ground turmeric*

*500 g (1 lb) mixed vegetables, such as carrots, courgettes, aubergines, beans and peppers*

*2 tablespoons vegetable oil*

*1 teaspoon cumin seeds*

*25 g (1 oz) desiccated coconut*

*salt to taste*

**For the 'final-fry':**

*2 tablespoons vegetable oil*

*½ teaspoon mustard seeds*

*¼ teaspoon ground asafoetida*

*2 whole dry red chillies*

*6 curry leaves*

*Kuttu is a must in south India even for festive occasions and is often served as the second course. It is commonly made with gourds, cluster beans, bananas, aubergines, beans, carrots, peppers, onions and pumpkins. I have suggested a combination but you can make up your own according to what is available. Freezing is not recommended.*

Put the lentils, two thirds of the water and the turmeric in a large pan and bring it to the boil. Cover and simmer till the lentils are soft, about 15 minutes. Remove from the heat and keep aside. Meanwhile, cut the vegetables into bite-size pieces. In a wok or pan, heat the oil and gently fry the cumin seeds and desiccated coconut. Add the vegetables, the remaining water and salt to taste. Mix well and cook till the vegetables are nearly done according to your taste. Add the lentils and cook for 5 more minutes. While the vegetables are cooking, heat the oil for the 'final-fry' in a small frying pan. When it is nearly smoking-hot, add the seasoning ingredients and when the mustard seeds begin to crackle pour the oil and spices over the Kuttu, standing well back, and cover the pan with the lid immediately, to retain the aroma.

*Note:* In India, tamarind juice is added when the vegetables are being cooked. For this dish, however, I find lemon juice a good substitute: add it to taste, just before serving. The dish should have a fair amount of gravy and I like to garnish it with deep-fried peanuts. Kuttu can also be prepared without the dhal, as it is in India for any ordinary family meal.

# BAGARE BAINGAN

Richly-spiced aubergines                                    Serves 4–6

Preparation time: 30 minutes + 40–50 minutes cooking

|  |
|---|
| 1 small onion, sliced |
| 4 tablespoons desiccated coconut, browned |
| 1 teaspoon sesame seeds |
| 1 teaspoon poppy seeds |
| ½ teaspoon coriander seeds |
| 4 whole dry red chillies |
| 6 curry leaves |
| 5 cm (2-inch) piece of fresh ginger, crushed |
| 4 cloves of garlic, crushed |
| a handful of coriander leaves |
| 5 whole green chillies |
| 275 g (9 oz) small aubergines |
| 2 tablespoons sesame oil |
| 2 tablespoons vegetable oil |
| ½ teaspoon cumin seeds |
| 4 tablespoons tamarind juice |
| salt to taste |

*I think originally this dish was introduced to us by the Moghuls, but through the years the Deccani Muslims have adapted it a little by increasing the number of chillies. This is a festive dish. Choose small aubergines or try the egg-shaped ones.*

Dry-roast and blend the onion; desiccated coconut; sesame, poppy and coriander seeds; red chillies; curry leaves; ginger; garlic; coriander leaves and one green chilli. Make two deep cuts in the aubergines, leaving the four sections held together by the stem; make more than two cuts if using large aubergines. Rub a little of the ground paste into each aubergine and keep aside (do not allow them to stand too long before cooking or they will discolour).

In a wok or large pan heat the oils and fry the cumin seeds. Slit the remaining four green chillies down one side and add them to the pan, de-seeding them if wished. Fry for a few minutes, add the aubergines and quickly fry them on a high heat on all sides for a few minutes. Remove only the aubergines and keep them aside. In the same oil, fry the remaining ground paste with a few drops of water. Cook until the water has evaporated and the oil has separated from the ground paste. Return the aubergines to the wok or pan and allow them to simmer covered, until nearly cooked, about 15 minutes. Add the tamarind juice and stir gently to avoid damaging the aubergines. Continue to simmer until the aubergines are fully cooked and the oil has risen above the gravy. Serve hot.

This dish improves with time and I recommend you prepare it 24 hours before serving it.

# KEERAI

Spinach curry                                          Serves 4–6

Preparation time: 25 minutes

---

500 g (1 lb) fresh spinach or
250 g (8 oz) frozen spinach

4 tablespoons vegetable oil

1 teaspoon cumin seeds

4 whole dry red chillies

1 large onion, sliced thickly

4 cloves of garlic, crushed

salt to taste

**To garnish:**

1 tomato, chopped

---

*India is blessed with over a dozen varieties of green leafy vegetables and at least one is included daily. Try out Indian sorrel (ambat), dill (soova), red sorrel (chukkay) or Swiss chard in this recipe.*

Pick and wash the spinach leaves, chop them finely and leave them in a colander to drain. If you are using frozen leaves, chop them and leave them to drain in the same way.

Heat the oil in a wok or a large frying pan and fry the cumin seeds and red chillies until the chillies turn a dark colour. Add the onion and garlic and fry until they become a little soft. Add salt to taste and then the spinach. Mix well and cook till the spinach is done, 10–15 minutes. Do not allow the spinach to overcook and become discoloured. Garnish with chopped tomato and serve hot with rice and a lentil curry.

*Note:* Spinach is often combined with meat in India. After cooking Attu Erachi Kari (Madras meat curry, page 46) or Kothu Erachi Kari (Tamil Nadu mince, page 40) add chopped spinach and cook until the spinach is done.

*Keerai (Spinach curry)*

*Bagare Baingan*
*(Richly-spiced aubergines)*

*Aviyal (Mixed*
*vegetables in yogurt)*

# AVIYAL

Mixed vegetables in yogurt                                    Serves 4–6

Preparation time: 45 minutes

175 ml (6 fl oz) water

500 g (1 lb) mixed
vegetables prepared and cut
into bite-size pieces

4 tablespoons desiccated
coconut

2 cloves of garlic

3 fresh green chillies, or
more to taste, de-seeded if
wished

1 teaspoon cumin seeds

1 teaspoon salt

½ a green mango or a small
lime, sliced

4 curry leaves

150 g (5.29 oz) carton
natural yogurt

*This is a variation on the Tamil Nadu Kuttu (page 70). A similar combination of vegetables is used but dhal is not added, nor is the 'final-fry' necessary for this dish, as the flavours are brought out by the yogurt and coconut. Green mango is used in India but you can use a small lime. Using a slightly older yogurt will improve the flavour of this dish.*

Bring the water to the boil in a heavy pan and then add the vegetables and simmer until they are half-cooked. Meanwhile, blend the coconut, garlic, chillies, cumin seeds and salt together. Reduce the heat under the vegetables and add this paste, the mango or lime and the curry leaves. Remove the pan from the heat and allow the vegetables to cool until tepid. Beat the yogurt until smooth and fold it into the vegetables, mixing well to avoid curdling. Return the pan to a low heat and simmer until the vegetables are fully done, stirring regularly to avoid curdling. Serve hot. Aviyal does not freeze well.

*Note:* In India, this is prepared at temples and offered to the residing deities and then to the pilgrims. Just before serving, 5 tablespoons of raw coconut oil are added to enhance the flavour further: do try it.

# MASALA BHENDI

Spiced okra                                    Serves 4–6

Preparation time: 25 minutes

*250 g (8 oz) small firm tender okra*

*1 teaspoon ground coriander*

*½ teaspoon ground turmeric*

*½ teaspoon chilli powder*

*2 tablespoons vegetable oil*

*½ teaspoon cumin seeds*

*¼ teaspoon mustard seeds*

*a pinch of ground asafoetida*

*½ teaspoon sugar*

*juice of ½ lemon*

*salt to taste*

*In India, okra is known as 'ladies fingers'. Okra needs quick cooking, otherwise the texture becomes rather glutinous. This recipe is a dry one. You could also try okra left whole, rubbed with salt, chilli powder and ground turmeric and deep-fried until brown and crisp. I often serve deep-fried okra with liquid lentil dishes.*

Wash the okra and pat them dry. Top and tail them sparingly and then cut them into 5 mm (¼-inch) thick rounds. Mix the coriander, turmeric and chilli powder in a mixing bowl and toss the okra in the spices to coat them evenly. Heat the oil in a wok or a large frying pan and fry the cumin and mustard seeds and the asafoetida until the mustard seeds crackle. Reduce the heat and add the sugar and salt to taste. Add the okra with the spices and fry on a high heat for 3–4 minutes, stirring constantly. Sprinkle the lemon juice over the okra and serve hot. If you like garnish it with some desiccated coconut and coriander leaves as well. Do not freeze.

# IMHASA

Jewish-style stuffed vegetables                                    Serves 4–6

Preparation time: 50 minutes + 25 minutes cooking

500 g (1 lb) potatoes, peeled

6 green tender cabbage leaves

6 large spinach leaves, stems removed

4 medium-ripe tomatoes

1 tablespoon vegetable oil

1 teaspoon cumin seeds

3 green chillies, de-seeded if wished and chopped finely

4 cloves of garlic, crushed

250 g (8 oz) frozen peas, thawed and drained

oil for greasing

125 ml (4 fl oz) tamarind juice

salt to taste

**Oven temperature:**
Gas Mark 4/180°C/350°F

*Another elegant yet simple dish which the Ezekial family prepared for me in Mercara. I have followed their method but instead of stuffed onion petals I have used fresh spinach leaves. You can also try this with chicory, red cabbage, radicchio or chinese leaves. Freezing is not recommended.*

Preheat the oven. Boil the potatoes until tender, about 20 minutes, and mash them coarsely. Meanwhile, blanch the cabbage and spinach leaves separately for 1 minute in boiling water and refresh them in cold water to preserve the colour. Drain them and lay them flat to dry on a clean tea towel. Remove the tops of the tomatoes and scoop out the seeds, reserving them for the stuffing. Heat the oil in a wok or a large frying pan and fry the cumin seeds, green chillies and garlic until the garlic is golden brown. Add the potatoes, peas, salt to taste and the tomato seeds and mix well. Remove from the heat and allow to cool a little.

Take one cabbage leaf and place some stuffing in the centre. Fold in the edges and roll it up if necessary and place the parcel on a greased oven-proof dish. Place the open end downwards to stop the parcel opening. Repeat with the remaining cabbage leaves and do the same for the spinach leaves. Arrange the spinach packages in the dish away from the cabbage parcels, allowing space for the tomatoes. Fill the tomatoes with the stuffing and put them in the centre. Pour the tamarind juice into the baking dish, cover it with foil and bake it for 20–30 minutes. Serve hot with Hamim Broth (Jewish-style stuffed chicken, page 35).

*Imhasa (Jewish-style stuffed vegetables)*
*Masala Bhendi (Spiced okra)*

# ACCOMPANIMENTS

Accompaniments like chutneys, *pacchhadis* and pickles bring out the flavour of main courses. Chutneys and pickles enhance mild dishes and *pacchhadis*, which are cooling mixtures of yogurt, herbs and vegetables, subdue spicy ones. Chutneys do not have a lengthy storage life as pickles do, and in India a chutney is prepared each day in accordance with the menu.

There is an Indian belief that newly pregnant girls crave hot and sour pickles, and when a girl is found eating pickles in secret the family knows a happy event is ahead. It is customary that portions of pickles should be removed from storage jars before the sun sets. To prolong the life of a pickle, always use a clean, dry spoon and re-seal the bottle or jar well. Never return unused pickles to the jar.

*Pacchhadi* is not an easily recognisable name in the west, as Indian restaurants and recipes always use the term *raitha*. As this is a south Indian cookery book, however, allow me to introduce you to *pacchhadi*, a south Indian cousin of the north Indian *raitha*.

## TALI KATRIKAYA PACCHHADI

Fried aubergines in yogurt                                     Serves 4–6

Preparation time: 15 minutes + 1 hour chilling

*275 g (9 oz) aubergine, sliced and soaked in cold water for 30 minutes*

*4–6 tablespoons vegetable oil*

*1/4 teaspoon ground turmeric*

*1/2 teaspoon chilli powder*

*1 teaspoon salt*

*150 g (5.29 oz) carton of natural yogurt*

*This is a delightful combination and a very appetising accompaniment. It can also be served as a starter as I have done on several occasions.*

Drain the aubergine well and pat dry with a kitchen towel. Gently heat the oil in a frying pan and fry the aubergine slices with the turmeric, chilli powder and salt until they are a little crisp but not burnt, about 5–7 minutes. Fry on a high heat as aubergine tends to absorb oil very quickly. Beat the yogurt in a serving bowl and add salt to taste. Tuck the slices of aubergine into

**To garnish:**

*a few coriander or mint leaves*

the yogurt so part of the slices stick out and pour any remaining oil and spices over it. Garnish with coriander or mint leaves and chill for 1 hour. Do not freeze.

*Variations:* Vegetables suitable for this dish are boiled potato cubes, pepper slices, whole cooked okra, blanched cauliflower florets or boiled and chopped spinach leaves. To give more character to this *pacchhadi* you can also add cashew nuts as a garnish or sprinkle on coarsely chopped walnuts.

## HARA DHANIYA CHUTNEY

Fresh green coriander relish                                     Serves 4–6

Preparation time: 40 minutes + 1 hour chilling

*175–250 g (6–8 oz) fresh coriander leaves and tender stems*

*3 green chillies, de-seeded if wished*

*½ fresh coconut, grated or 50 g (2 oz) desiccated coconut*

*5 cm (2-inch) piece of fresh ginger, chopped*

*juice of 1 lemon*

*1 teaspoon salt*

*1 teaspoon sugar*

*2 tablespoons vegetable oil*

*a pinch of ground asafoetida*

*1 teaspoon mustard seeds*

*4 curry leaves, chopped coarsely*

*After Alle Chutney (Ginger relish, page 80), this is the most popular chutney and in most homes in India it is prepared on a daily basis. I always have batches in the freezer. It is delicious as a sandwich spread with slices of cucumber, and if you add ½ teaspoon of this chutney to lamb stews it will greatly enhance the flavour.*

Wash the coriander leaves and stems to remove any soil. Drain them well and then place them on a kitchen towel to remove any excess water. Place the first seven ingredients in an electric food processor and blend them smoothly: you may need to move the leaves with a spatula occasionally to facilitate blending; if necessary add more lemon juice. Remove to a serving dish. Heat the oil in a frying pan and fry the asafoetida, mustard seeds and curry leaves until the mustard seeds crackle. Pour the oil and spices over the chutney, cover the dish and leave it for 5 minutes. Mix well, adjust the seasoning and add lemon juice if necessary, and serve chilled.

*Note:* If you have access to one, add a small green mango, peeled and sliced, instead of lemon juice and use a minimum amount of water to facilitate blending the ingredients.

# ALLE CHUTNEY

Ginger relish | Serves 4–6

Preparation time: 15 minutes

50 g (2 oz) fresh ginger

3 cloves of garlic

25 g (1 oz) fresh coconut or 2 tablespoons desiccated coconut

2 green chillies, de-seeded if wished

½ teaspoon salt, or to taste

1 teaspoon sugar

150 g (5.29 oz) carton of natural yogurt, beaten

2 tablespoons vegetable oil

6 curry leaves

¾ teaspoon mustard seeds

2 whole dry red chillies

*This is a Coorg-style chutney which is not only delicious as an accompaniment to any meal but aids digestion as well. It will keep for up to three days in the refrigerator, but should not be frozen.*

Blend the ginger, garlic, coconut, green chillies, salt and sugar to a paste in an electric blender. Remove the paste and mix with the yogurt. Keep aside.

Heat the oil in a small frying pan and fry the curry leaves, mustard seeds and red chillies until the seeds crackle and the chillies are dark in colour. Cool a little and pour the oil and spices over the coconut and yogurt mixture. Mix well and serve cold.

*Alu Sag (Potato curry)*

*Nimbu Achar (Lime pickle)*

*Alle Chutney (Ginger relish)*

*Hara Dhaniya Chutney
(Fresh green coriander relish)*

*Thenga Chutney
(Coconut relish)*

# THENGA CHUTNEY

Coconut relish                                        Serves 4–6

Preparation time: 25 minutes

*2 tablespoons vegetable oil*

*2 tablespoons chick-peas or channa dhal*

*4 green chillies, de-seeded if wished and chopped*

*8 curry leaves*

*½ a fresh coconut, grated*

*1 teaspoon mustard seeds*

*a pinch of ground asafoetida*

*juice of 1 lemon*

*salt to taste*

*Coconut is used a great deal in south Indian cookery, as coconut trees grow luxuriously along the entire coast; it is said a tree can live up to two hundred years. The coconut tree is very sacred to the south Indians and they tend them like sons. It is also said that the coconut tree is endowed with a wonderful understanding of human voices and therefore grows best where children play and sing.*

Heat one tablespoon of oil in a frying-pan and fry the chick-peas, chillies and curry leaves until the chick-peas are golden-brown. Remove from the heat and allow to cool. Grind the fried ingredients, coconut and salt to taste in an electric blender and then transfer everything to a serving bowl. Heat the remaining oil and fry the mustard seeds and asafoetida until the seeds crackle. Pour the oil and spices over the chutney and mix well. Add the lemon juice and mix again. Cool and serve, or keep for 2–3 days.

*Note:* Fresh coconut is best for this chutney, but you can use eight tablespoons of desiccated coconut soaked in four tablespoons of milk or buttermilk to soften it before it is ground.

# NIMBU ACHAR

Lime pickle                                  Makes two 250 g (8 oz) jars

Preparation time: 30 minutes + 10–15 days maturing

*12 limes*

*75 g (3 oz) salt*

*25 g (1 oz) fenugreek seeds*

*25 g (1 oz) mustard seeds*

*50 g (2 oz) chilli powder, or more to taste*

*1 tablespoon ground turmeric*

*This is definitely my favourite pickle and it makes a delicious accompaniment to any meal, even a cheese sandwich. You can also use thin-rinded lemons.*

Cut each lime into six sections and remove the pips if you wish. Place the limes in a large sterilised jar or glass bowl. Cover them with salt and leave them aside. Dry-roast the fenugreek and mustard seeds and then grind them to a fine

300 ml (½ pint) mustard oil or good quality vegetable oil

½ teaspoon ground asafoetida

powder. Add the ground seeds, chilli powder and ground turmeric to the limes and mix well. In a pan, heat the oil until it smokes and fry the asafoetida for 30 seconds. Pour the oil over the limes and mix well with a clean and dry wooden spoon. Cover the jar or bowl with a clean cloth and leave in a bright and warm place to rest till the limes are soft and a dull brown in colour, 10–15 days, depending on the warmth provided. I allow mine to rest close to the rear vent of the refrigerator or freezer where warm air is released. Stored in sterile, airtight jars, this pickle will keep indefinitely; do not freeze it though.

# ALU SAG

Potato curry                                                    Serves 4–6

Preparation time: 45 minutes

500 g (1 lb) potatoes, peeled

½ teaspoon ground turmeric

1 teaspoon salt

2 tablespoons vegetable oil

½ teaspoon mustard seeds

8 curry leaves, chopped

1 large onion or 8 spring onions, chopped finely

2 large firm tomatoes, chopped

½ teaspoon aniseed

½ teaspoon cumin seeds

5 large whole dry red chillies, de-seeded if wished

2 cloves of garlic

a little warm water, if necessary

juice of 1 lemon

**To garnish:**

chopped coriander

*The humble potato is prepared in a hundred or more ways devised for the table by the artistic Indians. In this south Indian method the potato is prepared to be served with Dosai (page 18) and accompanied by coconut chutney, or try it as a sandwich filling. Freezing is not recommended.*

Place the potatoes in a large pan with the turmeric and salt and cover them with water. Bring to the boil and cook till they are nearly done, 10–15 minutes. Drain them and when cool enough to handle chop them coarsely. In a wok or a large pan heat the oil and fry the mustard seeds till they crackle. Reduce the heat and add the curry leaves, onion and tomatoes and stir-fry until the onion is translucent. Blend the aniseed, cumin seeds, chillies and garlic to a fine paste, add this to the frying pan and fry until aromatic. Add the potatoes and mix well. Sprinkle on a little warm water if too dry. Sauté for a few minutes. Add the lemon juice and garnish just before serving.

# MANGAI ACHAR

| Mango pickle | Makes two 250 g (8 oz) jars |
| --- | --- |

Preparation time: 15 minutes + 30 minutes cooking

6 medium-size, unripe
mangoes

275 ml (9 fl oz) mustard oil
or good quality vegetable oil

½ teaspoon ground
asafoetida

125 g (4 oz) dry red chillies,
broken coarsely

1 teaspoon fenugreek seeds

2 tablespoons mustard seeds

1 tablespoon ground turmeric

2 teaspoons salt, or to taste

*Mangai Achar*
*(Mango pickle)* ➤

*Kirakai Pudina Pacchhadi*
*(Yogurt with cucumber*
*and mint)*

*The west finds it strange that in India, particularly the south where the climate is very hot, extremely hot foods like pickles are eaten. One good reason is that we believe they increase the appetite and aid digestion. Each region boasts its own variation but I have chosen one from Tamil Nadu. This method involves cooking, but in India the popular varieties are salted and sun-dried and have a storage life of two years or more. This stores indefinitely, but freezing is not recommended. It is a very hot recipe, so you may want to adjust the quantities to suit you, and use only a tiny amount at a time.*

Wash the mangoes and dry them well. Cut them into small pieces, including the stone, which will become soft when cooked, but pull out the kernel with a fork. Heat two tablespoons of oil in a small frying pan and fry the asafoetida, chillies and fenugreek seeds on a low heat until the fenugreek seeds swell. Remove, cool and grind to a paste with the oil. Heat the remaining oil in a large pan and when it is nearly smoking add the mustard seeds and fry them till they crackle. (Keep a window open if you are using mustard oil, as the smoke will sting your eyes.) Add the mangoes, ground turmeric and salt. Reduce the heat and cook until the mangoes are tender, 25–30 minutes. Cool completely and store for at least seven days before use.

# KIRAKAI PUDINA PACCHHADI

| Yogurt with cucumber and mint | Serves 4–6 |
| --- | --- |

Preparation time: 15 minutes + 1 hour chilling

150 g (5.29 oz) carton of
natural yogurt

*Yogurt combined with vegetables, spices, herbs and fruits is called 'pacchhadi' or 'raitha' and should be served with any main course. Use a set type of yogurt*

½ small cucumber, sliced thinly

20 mint leaves, chopped finely

2 green chillies, de-seeded if wished and chopped finely

1 tablespoon vegetable oil

½ teaspoon mustard seeds

salt to taste

**To garnish:**

fresh mint leaves

*for preference. I use scissors to cut up the mint leaves very finely.*

Beat the yogurt until smooth and fold in the cucumber, mint leaves, chillies and salt to taste. In a frying pan heat the oil and fry the mustard seeds until they crackle. Pour the oil and mustard seeds over the yogurt and cover without mixing in. Chill in the refrigerator for 1 hour. Before serving, mix the oil and mustard seeds into the yogurt and garnish with a few whole mint leaves. Do not freeze.

*Variations:* Raw vegetables suitable to serve in this manner are radishes, carrots, cauliflowers, tomatoes, peppers and onions.

Plain *pacchhadi* can also be served. Heat the oil and fry ½ teaspoon mustard seeds, 1 coarsely broken dry red chilli and a pinch of ground turmeric. When the seeds crackle pour over the yogurt. Chill but do not fold the oil into the yogurt until you serve it. Garnish with coriander or mint leaves. Do not freeze.

## KACHOOMBAR

Onion and tomato salad (Pictured on page 5)                    Serves 4–6

Preparation time: 20 minutes + chilling

1 large onion, chopped finely

2 small firm tomatoes, chopped finely

2 green chillies, de-seeded if wished and chopped finely

a few coriander and mint leaves, chopped finely

juice of 1 lemon

¼ teaspoon salt

½ teaspoon sugar

*This is a Muslim accompaniment. Serve it with any meal and definitely if you have chosen a Muslim menu.*

Mix all the ingredients in a bowl and allow them to rest till the sugar dissolves. Serve chilled.

# SWEETS AND DRINKS

For daily meals a housewife does not customarily prepare a sweet and fresh fruit is preferred. For this chapter I have selected sweets that are mainly served on religious and auspicious occasions and must therefore be considered 'divine foods'. Indian sweets are generally milk-based, and ingredients like grains, fruits, flour and nuts are added. Even today cane sugar (*gur*) or palm sugar (*jaggery*) are used; refined sugar was only introduced to India during the Moghul era.

Sweets in India are so sweet that one can only eat token amounts. I have reduced the sugar in these recipes to make them suitable for western palates without ruining the authentic taste.

## SEVIYAN KA MUZZAFER

| Vermicelli pudding | Serves 4–6 |
|---|---|

Preparation time: 10 minutes + 40 minutes cooking

6 tablespoons concentrated butter or ghee

2 green cardamoms

250 g (8 oz) very fine vermicelli

3 tablespoons sugar, or to taste

125 g (4 oz) almond flakes

125 g (4 oz) sultanas

250 ml (8 fl oz) milk

250 ml (8 fl oz) water

a few strands of saffron, soaked

*On auspicious occasions, Muslims generally begin and end their meal with a sweet. A token amount is taken at the start of the meal and the remainder at the end.*

Gently heat the butter or ghee in a non-stick wok or pan and fry the cardamoms for 1 minute. Break the vermicelli coarsely and then fry until it is golden brown in colour. Add the remaining ingredients and mix well. Cook until the vermicelli is soft and all the liquid has been absorbed, up to 40 minutes. When the vermicelli is done and almost dry, the ghee or butter should begin to separate from the mixture. Serve the pudding hot or cold, topping it with whipped cream if you wish.

# MYSORE PAK

Gram flour sweet                                    Makes 8–10 pieces

Preparation time: 1 hour + 30 minutes setting

*275 g (9 oz) concentrated
butter or ghee, plus extra for
greasing*

*175 g (6 oz) gram flour*

*350 g (12 oz) sugar*

*75 ml (3 fl oz) water*

*A light, fudge-like sweet with a spongy texture.
Although time-consuming to make it is delicious and
worth the effort. This is very popular in the state of
Karnataka of which the capital is Mysore. It doesn't
freeze but can be stored for up to 10 days.*

Gently heat a tablespoon of butter or ghee in a
wok or a frying–pan and fry the gram flour for
5 minutes without browning it too much. Take
the pan from the heat and keep aside. Bring the
sugar and water to the boil in a heavy saucepan.
Stir, lower the heat and simmer until you have a
one–thread consistency, that is, when you touch
it one thread sticks to your fingers. While the
syrup is still simmering, gradually add the flour
and stir continuously. After 5 minutes of stirring
begin adding the remaining butter or ghee about
two tablespoons at a time. Keep stirring and
when the ghee or butter has been used up in this
manner allow the mixture to reach boiling
point. Continue stirring all the time and when
the mixture is frothy and the ghee or butter
begins to separate from the flour and syrup pour
it on to a greased 20 × 20 cm (8 × 8-inch) baking
tin and spread it out evenly with a greased
spatula; leave to set for 30 minutes. Cut into
decorative shapes while still warm and allow the
tin to rest tilted, to drain off some of the excess
butter or ghee.

*Mysore Pak (Gram flour sweet)
Seviyan Ka Muzzafer (Vermicelli pudding)
Pal Payasam (Rice pudding)*

# PAL PAYASAM

Rice pudding                                    Serves 4–6

Preparation time: 1½ hours + 2 hours chilling

75 g (3 oz) long grain or
pudding rice

750 ml (1¼ pints) milk

175 ml (6 fl oz) water

4 tablespoons sugar, or to
taste

½ teaspoon ground
cardamom or nutmeg

a few strands of saffron
soaked in 1 tablespoon
warm milk or water

**To garnish:**

flaked almonds

pink rose petals

*A very popular sweet which Hindus call 'payasam'
and the Muslims call 'kheer'. When prepared by
Hindus it is first offered to Lord Krishna and only
cow's milk is used. Rice payasam is the most common
version but payasams are also made with sago, fruits,
lentils and vegetables like sweet potato.*

Wash the rice and dry it well on a kitchen towel
and then pound it until the grains are coarsely
broken. In a large, deep pan which will hold
twice the volume of the milk, bring the milk to
the boil. Reduce the heat a little and allow the
milk to froth continuously but not to bubble
over. Keep stirring from time to time so the milk
does not scorch and keep cooking till the milk is
reduced by half, about 40 minutes. Add the rice
and the water and cook, uncovered, until the rice
becomes soft, about 30 minutes. The texture
will grow quite thick. Add the sugar, cardamom
or nutmeg and saffron and cook until the sugar
dissolves, about 10 minutes. Pour into serving
dishes. Chill for about 2 hours and serve
decorated with almond flakes. In India, pink
rose petals are also used.

*Variations:* Use a teaspoon of rose-water
instead of cardamom or nutmeg and flavour with
two bay leaves, which should be added with the
rice and removed before serving. This payasam
is eaten on its own or with Poories (page 23).

# FALUDA

Gelatine pudding (Pictured on page 5)            Serves 4–6

Preparation time: 24 hours soaking + 40 minutes cooking + 1 hour

25 g (1 oz) china grass or
agar-agar or 11 g (½ oz)
sachet of gelatine

75 ml (3 fl oz) water

*China grass, a natural setting agent extracted from
seaweed, or agar-agar is used to set this pudding but
you can substitute one gelatine sachet, following the
instructions on the packet.*

600 ml (1 pint) milk

3 tablespoons granulated sugar, or to taste

1 teaspoon rose essence or rose-water or 2 drops kewra

a few drops of red food colouring

**To decorate:**

rose petals

crushed cardamom seeds

Soak the china grass or agar-agar in the water overnight. Boil the milk and sugar until the sugar dissolves and set the pan aside. Boil the china grass or agar-agar until it dissolves. Mix it with the milk and rose essence or rose-water or kewra. Divide into two equal parts. To one part add a few drops of red food colour to obtain a pinky shade. Keep the pink portion warm to prevent it from setting. Whisk the white portion until frothy. Pour it into a glass dish and leave to set for 30 minutes. When it is set, cool the pink portion very slightly and pour it in on top of the white. Allow the pink portion to set above the white portion for 30 minutes. Chill in the refrigerator and serve decorated with rose petals and crushed cardamom seeds. Do not freeze.

*Variations:* Flavour with coffee essence and chocolate colouring; banana essence and yellow colouring; almond essence and green colouring; almond essence and saffron strands.

# PAZHA PAYASAM

Banana milk pudding                                    Serves 4–6

Preparation time: 35 minutes + 20 minutes cooking

3 tablespoons concentrated butter or ghee

4 ripe bananas, sliced

175 ml (6 fl oz) water

175 g (6 oz) soft light brown sugar

50 g (2 oz) creamed coconut dissolved in 350 ml (12 fl oz) hot water

¼ teaspoon ground ginger

¼ teaspoon ground cardamom or nutmeg

*This is a Kerala speciality. Because of the abundance of coconut palms in Kerala coconut milk is preferred for their payasams.*

Gently heat the butter or ghee in a heavy pan (preferably a non-stick one) and fry the bananas for about 10 minutes. Mash the fruit with a fork or potato masher. Add the water and simmer for a further 10 minutes or until the fruit is thoroughly cooked. Add the sugar and mix well. Simmer till the sugar dissolves and you have a thick syrupy consistency. Add the coconut milk and simmer for another 20 minutes. Fold in the spices and serve hot or cold. Do not freeze.

# AAMB KA HALWA

Mango bites                                                 Serves 4–6

Preparation time: 45 minutes

500 g (1 lb) mango pulp

450 ml (¾ pint) milk

175 g (6 oz) sugar, or to taste

¼ teaspoon ground cardamom

*The best variety of mango pulp is that of Alfonso mangoes. Sweetened and unsweetened varieties are available so check the labels carefully. Alternatively, drain canned mango slices and blend them to a pulp.*

Put all the ingredients in a large pan and allow the mixture to cook on a low heat. Stir continuously as it is prone to stick. When the mixture leaves the sides of the pan it is done, about 45 minutes. Grease a tray, pour the mixture into it and allow it to set, about 30 minutes. Cut into diamond shapes when cold. Do not freeze.

# PHAL MAVA

Indian fruit salad                                          Serves 4–6

Preparation time: 20 minutes + chilling

1 small honeydew melon

2 medium-ripe bananas

2 fresh mangoes, peeled and sliced or 400 g (14 oz) can of mango slices, drained

2 oranges, peeled and segmented

a few green and black grapes, de-seeded

2 tablespoons sugar, or to taste

¼ teaspoon salt

¼ teaspoon black pepper

juice of 1 lime or lemon

**To decorate:**

mint leaves (optional)

*During the mango season this 'mava' is offered to the deity Balaji in his temples in Hyderabad and Tirupathi.*

Cut the melon into 2.5 cm (1-inch) pieces or scoop the flesh into balls. Slice the bananas diagonally. Mix all the ingredients together in a glass serving dish and decorate with mint leaves if wished. Chill thoroughly and serve. Do not freeze.

*Phal Mava (Indian fruit salad)*
*Aamb Ka Halwa (Mango bites)*

# MOR

Preparation time: 20 minutes + 4 hours chilling

| |
|---|
| 1.2 litres (2 pints) buttermilk |
| 1 green chilli, chopped finely |
| 1 small onion, chopped finely |
| a few mint or coriander leaves, chopped finely |
| 1 teaspoon salt, or to taste |
| ¼ teaspoon freshly ground black pepper |
| ¼ teaspoon freshly ground cumin or fennel seeds |

*The Hindus in south India must end their meal with yogurt or buttermilk. Buttermilk is prepared by churning yogurt, adding some water and then removing the fat in the form of butter. But you can just whisk the yogurt with water to make the consistency of a thick milk shake or use commercial buttermilk.*

Mix all the ingredients with a whisk. Chill thoroughly and serve. Do not freeze.

# LASSI OR CHANS

Preparation time: 10 minutes + 4–6 hours chilling

| |
|---|
| 1.2 litres (2 pints) buttermilk |
| 4 tablespoons sugar, or to taste |
| 1 teaspoon salt, or to taste |
| 1 teaspoon freshly ground black pepper |
| 1 teaspoon freshly ground cumin seeds |
| 1 teaspoon freshly ground fennel seeds |

*This is a Muslim variation of Mor (Savoury butter-milk, above), often served with the main meal and combined with dishes like pilaus and biryanis.*

Mix all the ingredients with a whisk, chill thoroughly and serve. Do not freeze.